Th.
Lib
w
I

Senior editor Chris Hawkes
Senior art editors Mik Gates, Stefan Podhorodecki
Editor Suhel Ahmed
Designers David Ball, Chrissy Barnard,
Kit Lane, Simon Mumford, Sadie Thomas
Illustrations Adam Benton, Stuart Jackson-Carter,
Jon@kja-artists
Creative retouching Steve Crozier
Picture research Nic Dean, Surya Sarangi

Senior jacket designer Mark Cavanagh
Jacket designers Tanya Mehrotra, Suhita Dharamjit
Jacket editor Claire Gell
Jackets editorial coordinator Priyanka Sharma
DTP designer Rakesh Kumar
Managing jackets editor Saloni Singh
Jacket design development manager
Sophia MTT
Consultant Tracey Bourne (Football Studies –
Southampton Solent University; FA Associate tutor)
Producer (pre-production) Jacqueline Street
Senior producer Gary Batchelor

Managing art editor Philip Letsu
Managing editor Francesca Baines
Publisher Andrew Macintyre
Art director Karen Self
Associate publishing director Liz Wheeler
Publishing director Jonathan Metcalf

First published in Great Britain in 2017
by Dorling Kindersley Limited
80 Strand, London, WC2R 0RL

A CIP catalogue record for this book
is available from the British Library.

ISBN: 978-0-2412-2822-7

Printed and bound in China

Discover more at
www.dk.com

CONTENTS

The beautiful game

Play to the whistle

Individual skills

A team game

Club world

Tournaments and trophies

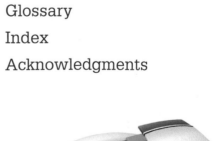

The beautiful game

No one knows who invented football. However, once the game's rules were set down, in 1863, it did not take long for football to reach every corner of the world. Today, it is the most popular sport on the planet, with around 3.5 billion fans.

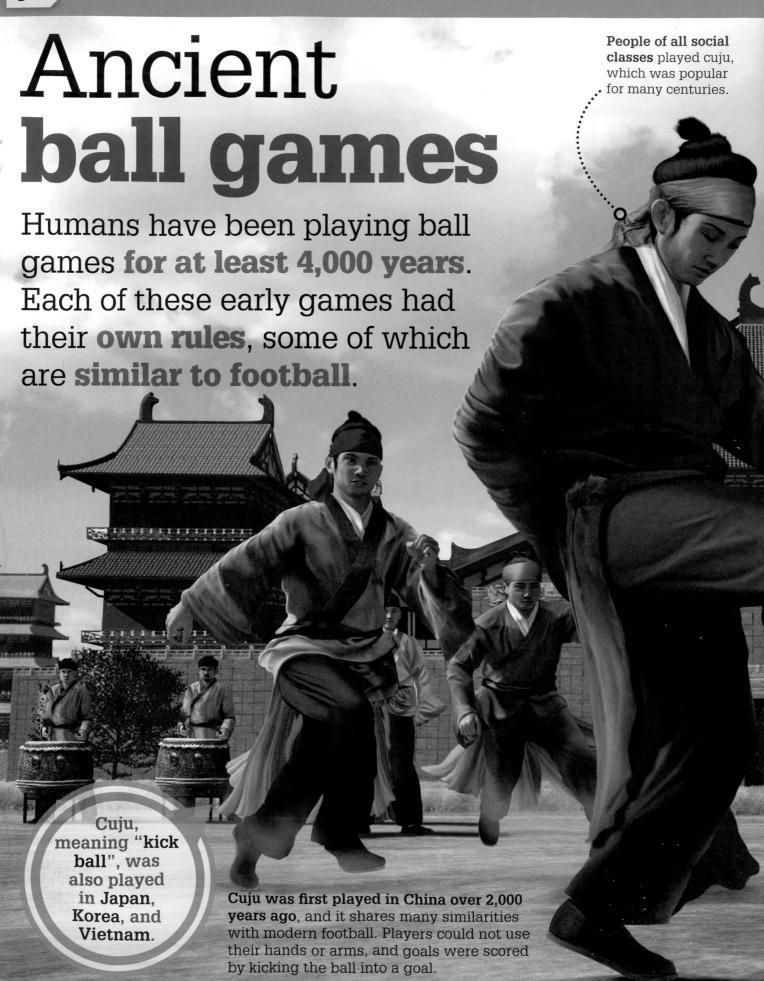

Ancient ball games

Humans have been playing ball games **for at least 4,000 years**. Each of these early games had their **own rules**, some of which are **similar to football**.

People of all social classes played cuju, which was popular for many centuries.

Cuju, meaning "kick ball", was also played in Japan, Korea, and Vietnam.

Cuju was first played in China over 2,000 years ago, and it shares many similarities with modern football. Players could not use their hands or arms, and goals were scored by kicking the ball into a goal.

MESOAMERICAN BALL GAME

Played in Central America 3,600 years ago, the Mesoamerican ball game is the world's oldest team sport. Players played on a court, could not use their hands, and scored goals by getting the ball to pass through a hoop.

A competitive match consisted of two teams of 12–16 players on each side.

Individual players attracted fame and fortune, and, by the 10th century, there was even a national championship to decide the best team.

The ball had an outer covering made of leather and was stuffed tightly with feathers.

Birth of football

A variety of football-like games were played in **English boarding schools** in the **mid-19th century**. However, **the rules** of these games were **so different** that it was virtually impossible for the school teams to play against each other.

Eight players make up the bully: three "corners", two "sideposts", one "post", one "pup", and one "fly".

Players outside the bully are called "behinds". Their role is to kick the ball over the bully towards the opponent's goal.

Behinds are made up of two types of player: "shorts" and "longs".

The rules for the **Eton Field Game** were first written down in 1815.

THE FOOTBALL ASSOCIATION (FA)

Englishman Ebenezer Cobb Morley could be called the father of the Football Association. His letter suggesting that football should have a common set of rules (meaning that teams could play against each other) led to a series of meetings that ended with the foundation of the Football Association on 26 October 1863. The game's first set of rules were published a few months later.

At the school of Eton, they played – and still do – the Field Game. As in football, the ball is round and players are not allowed to pick it up. However, the rules are more complicated than in football, and there is also a scrum, called a "bully".

FIRST INTERNATIONAL

The first international was played between England and Scotland in Glasgow, Scotland, in 1872. It finished 0–0.

Football spread to countries through the many connections of the British Empire, introduced by the huge number of British workers who travelled throughout the world. It did not take long before these countries started to form their own national football associations.

1863 The Football Association, football's first national governing body, is established in England.

1876 The Welsh FA is founded.

1891 New Zealand becomes the first country outside Europe to create a national football association.

1893 The first national football association in South America is established in Argentina.

1904 The Haiti Football Association is formed – the first in North America.

1921 Egypt becomes the first African country to create a national football association.

1924 The Chinese Football Association is founded.

1928 Israel and Palestine both create national associations.

1860

1873 Scotland forms the world's second national football association.

1890

1889 Denmark and the Netherlands become the first countries in continental Europe to create national associations.

1912 The Canadian Soccer Association is founded. The US Soccer Federation follows a year later.

1920

1939 By the start of World War II there were 109 national associations.

Football spreads around the world

Established in 1857, **Sheffield FC** is the **world's oldest** football club.

After the Football Association was established in England in 1863, it took **little more than a century** for football to appear in **every continent** and **nearly every country** in the world.

1947 A national association is created in newly formed Pakistan.

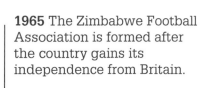

1965 The Zimbabwe Football Association is formed after the country gains its independence from Britain.

1971 The United Arab Emirates Football Association is formed in the same year the country is created.

1989 Belarus becomes the first former Soviet state to form its own national football association.

2011 South Sudan becomes the most recent country to form a national association.

1950

1980

2010

1960 Twelve national associations are formed around the world; the most in a single year.

1961 Football Federation Australia is formed, 70 years after its equivalent in New Zealand.

1991 The South African Football Association is reformed following the end of apartheid.

The modern era

The **Fédération Internationale de Football Association (FIFA)** is the game's international governing body. **Every continent**, with the exception of Antarctica, **has its own confederation**, which organizes international and club competitions.

CONCACAF

CONCACAF governs the game in North and Central America and the Caribbean. Its headquarters are in New York, USA.

Formed: 1961
Members: 41
Major tournaments:
International:
CONCACAF Gold Cup
Club: CONCACAF Champions League

UEFA

UEFA is the governing body of football in Europe. Its headquarters are located in Nyon, Switzerland.

Formed: 1954
Members: 55
Major tournaments:
International:
UEFA European
Championship;

Club: UEFA Champions League,
UEFA Europa League

CONMEBOL

The oldest of the continental confederations, CONMEBOL was formed in 1916. It governs football in South America and its headquarters are in Luque, Paraguay.

Formed: 1916
Members: 10
Major tournaments:
International: Copa América
Club: Copa Libertadores,
Copa Sudamericana

CAF

The CAF governs football in Africa and has more members than any other confederation. Its headquarters are in Cairo, Egypt.

Formed: 1957
Members: 56
Major tournaments:
International: Africa
Cup of Nations
Club: CAF Champions
League, CAF Confederation
Cup

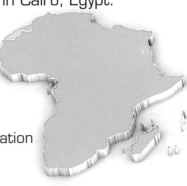

FIFA

FIFA is football's global governing body and organizes the game's major international tournaments. Its headquarters are in Zurich, Switzerland.

Formed: 1904
Members: 211
Major tournaments:
FIFA World Cup, FIFA Women's World Cup, FIFA Confederations Cup, Olympic Games

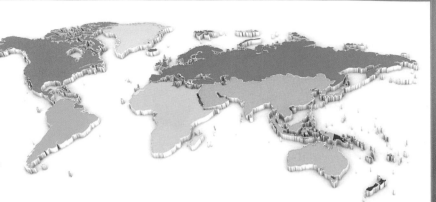

AFC

The AFC governs football in Asia and, since 2006, Australia, from its headquarters in Kuala Lumpur, Malaysia.

Formed: 1954
Members: 47
Major tournaments:
International:
AFC Asia Cup
Club: AFC Champions League, AFC Cup

FIFA's motto is: "For the game. For the world."

OFC

Founded in 1966, the OFC is the youngest of football's confederations. It governs the game in Oceania from its headquarters in Auckland, New Zealand.

Formed: 1966
Members: 14
Major tournaments:
International:
OFC Nations Cup
Club: Oceania Club Championship

CUT OFF IN ITS PRIME

By 1920, the women's game was as popular as the men's, with one match in England featuring Dick, Kerr's Ladies FC (above, right), attracting a crowd of 53,000. In 1921, however, the FA banned women's matches at their grounds, saying the sport was inappropriate for women.

1881 An unofficial women's international match is played between Scotland and England in Edinburgh on 7 May 1881. Scotland wins 3–0.

1890s Several women's clubs are formed in England. One match, in north London, attracted a crowd of 10,000.

1921 The Football Association bans women's teams from playing on association members' pitches.

1930s Women's leagues are established in France and Italy.

1881   1930

1919 The first-ever women's French Championship is played – only two teams take part.

1920 Dick, Kerr's Ladies, England's leading women's team, play a French XI team in France. They win the match 2–0, in front of a crowd of 62,000.

Women's football

Women's football has gone through many **ups and downs** over the years. Once as popular as the men's game, it was then **banned**, but it has enjoyed a **huge resurgence** in recent times.

Action from the 2015 FIFA Women's World Cup match between the Ivory Coast and Thailand (which Thailand won 3–2). The tournament, held in Canada, featured 24 teams for the first time and was shown on television in 171 countries.

1951 The first women's league is established in the United States.

1996 Women's football is included in the programme of events at the Olympic Games for the first time.

1984 Sweden win the first official UEFA Women's European Championship.

1971 The FA lifts its ban on women's football. The same year, UEFA recommends the women's game should be taken under the control of the national associations of each country.

2017 The number of national women's teams participating in international matches rises to 176.

1960   **1980**   **2000**

1969 A group of women's clubs form the Women's FA in England.

1989 Japan becomes the first country to launch a semi-professional women's league.

1991 The United States win the first FIFA Women's World Cup.

The first FIFA-approved women's international was played in **1971**.

1957 Germany organizes an unofficial women's European Championship.

Extra time

The **10 essentials** of the ancient Chinese game of **cuju** included: respect for other players, courtesy, *team spirit*, no ungentlemanly behaviour, no dangerous play, and no ball-hogging.

Balls in the **Mesoamerican ball game** from Central America varied; some were as small as **tennis balls**, while others could weigh up to 3.6 kg (8 lb) – that's the same weight as a **watermelon**.

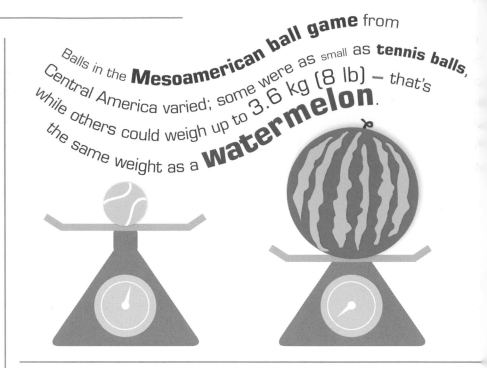

80 per cent of FIFA member associations have a **senior women's team.**

1,166,926 girls around the world play in grassroots football programmes.

Countries with the most registered players

If a player plays for a club, they are normally registered with their national football association. The graphic below shows the countries with the most registered players (female and male).

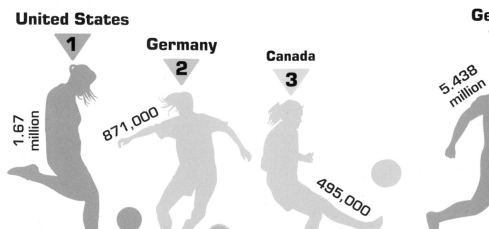

United States
▼ 1
1.67 million

Germany
▼ 2
871,000

Canada
▼ 3
495,000

Female players

Germany
▼ 1
5.438 million

United States
▼ 2
2.517 million

Brazil
▼ 3
2.115 million

Male players

The world's richest leagues

Football leagues make the majority of their money by selling the rights to show games to television companies. The world's top-five richest leagues are all in Europe, with England's Premier League at the top.

Premier League England
€ 4.07 billion

Bundesliga Germany
€ 3.24 billion

Ligue 1 France
€ 1.418 billion

Serie A Italy
€ 1.792 billion

La Liga Spain
€ 2.417 billion

50 per cent

of FIFA member association countries have a **youth team**.

FIFA has 211 members, compared with the United Nation's 193.

Countries with the most players

In 2007, FIFA conducted a survey to find out which countries had the most football players (registered and unregistered). Here are the top eight.

India 20.588 million

China 26.166 million

United States 24.473 million

Brazil 13.198 million

Germany 16.309 million

Mexico 8.48 million

Indoneisia 7.1 million

Nigeria 6.7 million

Play to the whistle

Anyone can play football: all you need is a ball and a space to play. Even the professional game is relatively simple: two teams of 11 players play for 90 minutes, while three match officials (the referee and the assistant referees) ensure that both teams play to the Laws of the Game.

Laws of the Game

Football has **17 laws** that cover every aspect of the game. The **English FA** devised 13 of these in 1863. The remaining four were added later on.

5 The referee
An appointed referee, whose decisions are final, are in charge of the match.

6 Assistant referees
Two officials are appointed to support the referee to enforce the rules.

7 Match duration
A match is played over two periods of 45 minutes each.

5. The referee

1 Field of play
The pitch size may vary, but must be rectangle, with the correct markings.

1. Field of play

1863

1891

1937

2 The ball
The ball must weigh 400–450 g (14–16 oz) and be about 22 cm (8.65 in) in diameter.

3 Number of players
A team has 11 players. A match cannot take place with fewer than seven players in a team.

3. Number of players

4 Players' equipment
Players must wear a jersey, shorts, socks, shin pads, and football boots.

The original "Laws of the Game" were handwritten by Ebenezer Cobb Morley in 1863.

8 **Start/restart of play**
A kick-off starts play, and restarts the game after a goal.

9 **Ball in play**
The ball is always in play unless the referee stops the game.

10 **Method of scoring**
A goal is scored when the whole of the ball crosses the goal line.

11 **Offside**
A player is offside if he or she goes behind the line of opposing defenders before receiving the ball from a teammate.

12 **Fouls and misconduct**
Players must play the game fairly and safely, and will be penalized for any unfair or unsporting behaviour.

13 **Free kick**
A team wins a free kick for any foul or offence committed against them. It is taken from the spot where the offence occurred.

14 **Penalty kick**
A team wins a penalty kick for any foul committed by an opponent in the opposition's own penalty area.

15 **Throw-in**
A team wins a throw-in when the ball crosses the touchline after touching an opposition player last.

16 **Goal kick**
The defending team wins a goal kick if the ball crosses their own goal line after touching an opposition player last.

17 **Corner kick**
The attacking team wins a corner if a defending player touches the ball last before it crosses the byline.

10. Method of scoring

12. Fouls and misconduct

15. Throw-in

17. Corner kick

I.
The maximum **length of the ground** shall be 200 yards, the maximum ...dth shall be 100 yards, the length and breadth shall be marked off with flags; the goal shall be defined by two upright posts, 8 ... apart, without any tap... across them.

II.
The Game shall be commenced by a place kick from the centre of ...ound by the side winning the toss, the other side ... approach within 10 yard... ...e ball until it is kicked off. After a goal is wo... ...e side shall be entitled to ...ff.

III.
The two sides shall change goals after each ... won.

IV.
A goal shall be won when the ball passe... ...the space between the goal post... ...atever height), not being thrown, knocke... ...or carried.

V.
When the ball is in **touch** the first pla... ...who touches it shall **kick** or throw it fro... ...t on the boundary line where it left ... ...ground, in a direction at right angles wi... ...ndary line.

VI.
A player shall be **out of play** i...mediately he is in front of the ball, and mu... ...behind the ball as soon as possible. If the ball is kicked past a player by his ow... ...e shall not touch or kick it or ...advance until one of the other side has first kicke... ...e of his own side on a level with or in front of him has been able to kick it.

VII.
In case the ball goes behind the goal line, if a player on the side to whom th... ...longs first touches the ball, one of his side shall be entitled to a free kick from th... ...e at the point opposite the place where the ball shall be touched. If a player ...osite side first touches the ball, one of his side shall be entitled to a free kick fro... ...15 yards outside the goal line, opposite the place where the ball is touched.

VIII.
If a player makes a **fair catch** he shall be entitled to a **free kick**, provided ...it by making a mark with his heel at once; and in order to take such kick he ma... ...ar back as he pleases, and no player on the oppos... side shall advance beyond ... ...ntil he has kicked.

IX.
A player shall be entitled to run with the ball towards his adversaries' goal if ... ...s fair catch, or catches the ball on the first bound; but in the case of a fair catch, ...es his mark, he shall not then run.

X.
If any player shall run with the ball towards his adversaries' goal, any player on th... ...e side shall be at liberty to charge, hold, trip, or hack him, or to wrest the ball fro... ...ut no player shall be held and hacked at the same time.

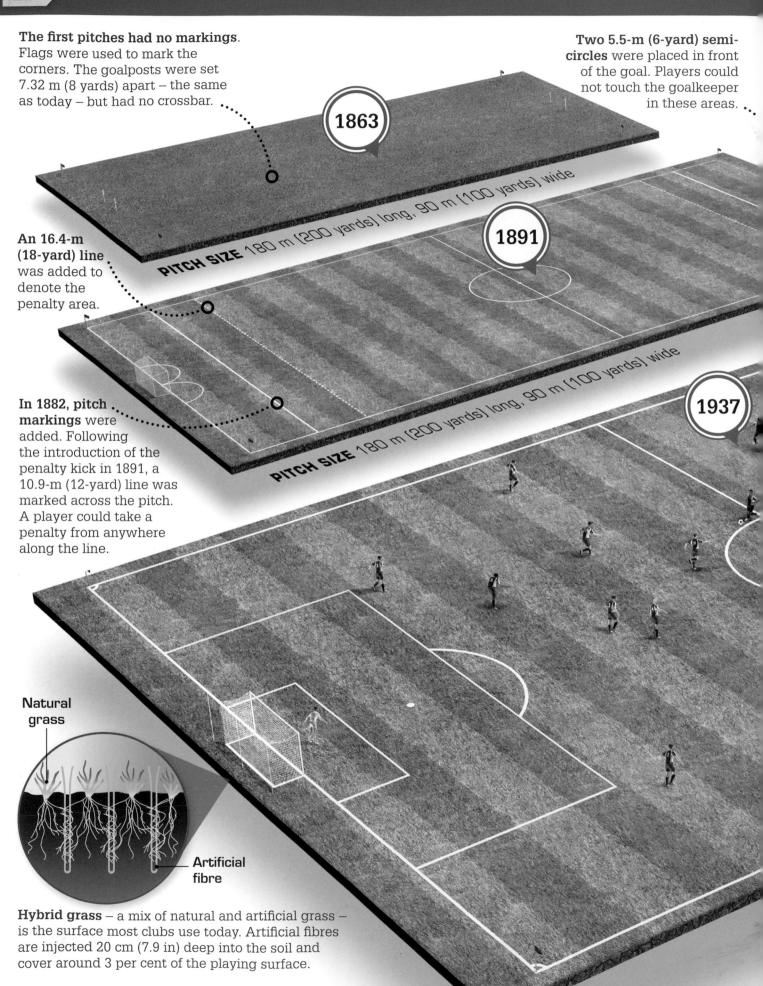

The first pitches had no markings. Flags were used to mark the corners. The goalposts were set 7.32 m (8 yards) apart – the same as today – but had no crossbar.

Two 5.5-m (6-yard) semi-circles were placed in front of the goal. Players could not touch the goalkeeper in these areas. ....

1863

PITCH SIZE 180 m (200 yards) long, 90 m (100 yards) wide

1891

An 16.4-m (18-yard) line was added to denote the penalty area.

PITCH SIZE 180 m (200 yards) long, 90 m (100 yards) wide

1937

In 1882, pitch markings were added. Following the introduction of the penalty kick in 1891, a 10.9-m (12-yard) line was marked across the pitch. A player could take a penalty from anywhere along the line.

Natural grass

Artificial fibre

Hybrid grass – a mix of natural and artificial grass – is the surface most clubs use today. Artificial fibres are injected 20 cm (7.9 in) deep into the soil and cover around 3 per cent of the playing surface.

The pitch

The FA's first rulebook contained no guidelines for pitch markings, and it was only in the early 20th century that football pitches began to take their modern form.

A tape was first hung between the goalposts in 1872. It was positioned 2.4 m (8 ft) above the ground. A solid crossbar replaced it in 1875.

The 16.4-m (18-yard) line was shrunk in 1902 to become the penalty area. The D, or arc, of the penalty area was added in 1937 to ensure players were at least 9 m (10 yards) from the penalty spot when a player took a penalty.

PITCH SIZE 90–120 m (100–120 yards) long, 45–90 m (50–100 yards) wide

A **standard pitch** contains an average of **300 million** blades of grass.

The size and appearance of a football pitch have changed since the game was first played in 1863. The illustrations above show just how much pitch markings have changed over the years.

UNDER-SOIL HEATING

Most clubs have under-soil heating systems beneath the playing surface. These consist of a vast network of tubes that contain hot water, which prevents the pitch from freezing over during the winter.

Inside a football

The **earliest footballs** were **inflated pig bladders** covered with leather. Ball technology has changed dramatically over the years, both in terms of **how balls are manufactured** and **what they are made of**.

Medieval footballers used a leather ball stuffed with an inflated pig's bladder, but this did not bounce well and often deflated. The modern ball has an outer cover made of synthetic leather, an inner lining to make it bouncy, and an inflated rubber bladder in the centre.

The oldest-known football was found in a Scottish castle. When analysed, it dated back to the 1540s.

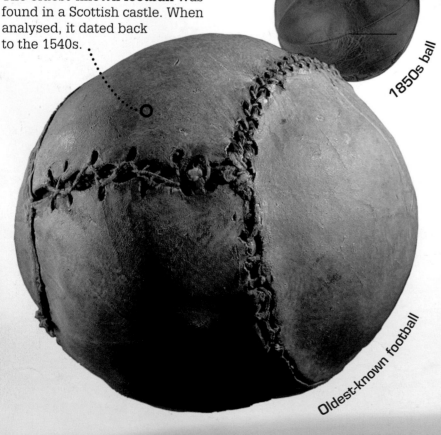

Oldest-known football

1970s buckyball

1990s ball

1880s ball

1850s ball

The buckyball consists of 20 hexagonal and 12 pentagonal panels stitched together.

📊 FAST FACTS

Footballs come in a range of standard sizes depending on the type of football being played and the age of the players.

Age: 14+

Size 5 ball
68.5–71 cm
(27–28 in)

Age: Under 14

Size 4 ball
63.5–66 cm
(25–26 in)

Age: Under 9

Size 3 ball
58.5–61 cm
(23–24 in)

Beach soccer ball
68.5–71 cm
(27–28 in)

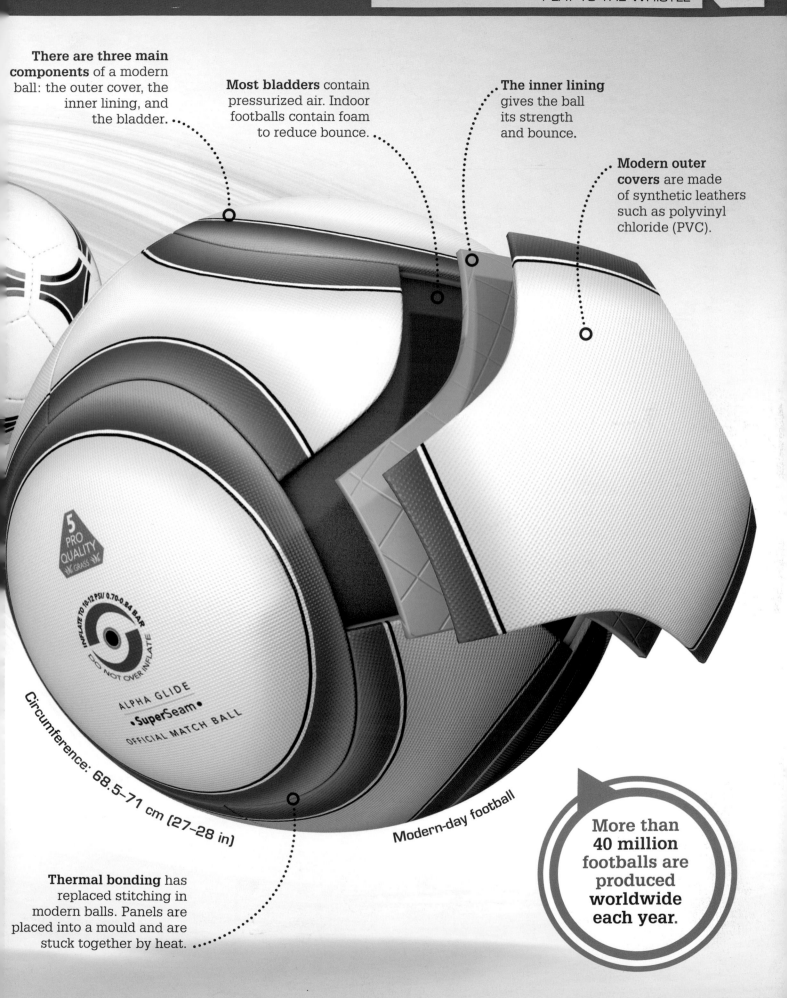

There are three main components of a modern ball: the outer cover, the inner lining, and the bladder.

Most bladders contain pressurized air. Indoor footballs contain foam to reduce bounce.

The inner lining gives the ball its strength and bounce.

Modern outer covers are made of synthetic leathers such as polyvinyl chloride (PVC).

5 PRO QUALITY GRASS

INFLATE TO 10-12 PSI/ 0.70-0.84 BAR

DO NOT OVER-INFLATE

ALPHA GLIDE

• SuperSeam •

OFFICIAL MATCH BALL

Circumference: 68.5–71 cm (27–28 in)

Modern-day football

Thermal bonding has replaced stitching in modern balls. Panels are placed into a mould and are stuck together by heat.

More than 40 million footballs are produced worldwide each year.

kitted out

Football kits have changed dramatically over the years, from the **thick cotton shirts** and **baggy shorts** of the 19th century, to the **hi-tech materials** used to make today's kits.

In 1921, the law was changed so that, in the event of a colour clash, the away team (and not the home team) had to change strip. Nowadays, all teams have a home kit and an away kit, with some teams also having a third kit.

Modern shirts are normally made of a polyester mesh that does not trap in heat or sweat. They also contain lycra, which adds strength and flexibility.

Sleeves can either be long or short according to the Laws of the Game.

Football kits are used to distinguish the two teams when they are on the pitch. Their design has changed hugely over the years. This illustration compares a kit from the 1890s to one worn by players today.

Early football shirts were made of thick cotton and had collars. Some team's shirts were even made of wool!

Team kits started to emerge in the 1870s.

Modern shorts are loose, which allows for freedom of movement and good air circulation.

Future shirts could contain computers that monitor a player's heart rate.

Modern shin pads are made of many different synthetic materials. They are designed to spread the load of any impact over as wide an area as possible.

Socks must entirely cover the shin pad.

Today

1890

Shorts had to cover the knees according to a Football Association rule passed in 1904.

The first player to wear shin pads was Nottingham Forest's Sam Weller Widdowson in 1874. He wore a pair of cut-down cricket pads strapped to the outside of his socks.

Socks worn by early players could be any colour. Clubs were not required to register the colour and design of their socks until 1937.

Perfect boots

Early football boots were designed to provide players with **both protection** and **grip on the pitch**. Nowadays, following years of development, the main function of the modern boot is to **improve a player's performance**.

The boot's surface contains peaks and troughs of varying sizes. These are designed to aid touch and ball control.

The upper part of the boot is flexible, which helps the player's movement.

Studs have been shaped like arrows. Tests show that this shape provides the best grip.

Modern boots are a product of detailed research into comfort, a player's movement, and which part of the foot comes into contact with the ball the most.

An elasticated, knitted collar aids movement, ensures the boot is more firmly attached to the foot, and is comfortable.

EARLY BOOTS

Early football boots were made of leather, were uncomfortable, and heavy. It was not until 1891 that the Football Association allowed boots to be fitted with studs.

The boot's sole is shaped to fit the foot perfectly.

The earliest-known football boots were worn by English king Henry VIII in 1526.

The boot's plastic sole is flexible to increase a player's mobility.

The position of the studs has been established after detailed research into a player's movement on the pitch.

Top-flight referees carry hi-tech equipment worth up to $4,500 onto the pitch. This figure does not include the goal-line technology system, which costs about $650,000 to install in the stadium.

A headset is used by the referee to communicate with the assistant referees. It is designed to ensure they can hear one another clearly – even inside a noisy stadium.

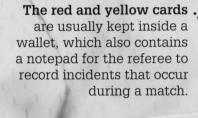

A two-way radio receiver relays the messages from the headset. The radio is powered by a battery pack.

The red and yellow cards are usually kept inside a wallet, which also contains a notepad for the referee to record incidents that occur during a match.

Before whistles, referees used handkerchiefs to draw the attention of players.

The goal-line technology (GLT) wrist device is linked to a computerized camera system, which monitors both goals and alerts the referee if the ball fully crosses either goal line.

The referee

The referee is responsible for **enforcing** the **Laws of the Game**. At elite level, referees are equipped with **state-of-the-art technology** to help them with their job.

The signal beep system buzzes and vibrates whenever either of the assistant referees presses a button on their flags. This alerts the referee to any infringement.

A stopwatch is used to keep track of the match time. At elite level, the watch also includes a heart-rate monitor to measure the referee's fitness level.

MARKER SPRAYS

When a team is awarded a free kick, the referee uses a foaming spray to create a temporary marker 9.1 m (10 yards) away from the kick. The defenders must stand behind the mark at the moment the free kick is taken.

A whistle is used to signal the start and restart of a match, to stop play due to a foul or injury, and to end each half.

An assistant referee **communicates** with the referee via a small radio set.

Assistant referees

Assistant referees help the referee **enforce the Laws of the Game.** One assistant referee runs along each touchline and is responsible for one half of the pitch. The **referee may overrule** any decision made by an assistant referee.

Assistant referees officiate in situations in which the referee is not ideally positioned to see an incident and make the best decision.

Assistant referees were **known as linesmen** before 1996.

A button on the flag is used to alert the referee instantly of any decision. This sends a beeping or vibrating signal to the referee.

The flag is brightly coloured to ensure it draws the referee's attention when the assistant referee makes a signal.

The Diagonal System

is the most common method used by referees to officiate in a game. The referee (R) patrols a diagonal line that runs from the opposite corners of each penalty area. Each assistant referee (AR) is responsible for a separate half of the pitch.

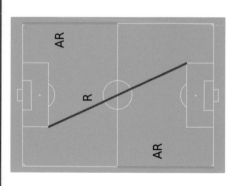

Assistant referees use a set of standard

flag signals to alert the referee to incidents and infringements that occur in their half of the pitch.

Substitution

A flag is held above the head with both hands to indicate a team's wish to make a substitution.

Offside

The flag is held above the head to signal for an offside offence.

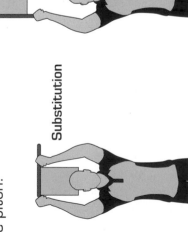

Throw-in

A flag is held out to one side, pointing in the direction of play of the team awarded the throw-in.

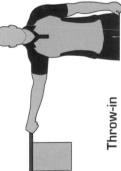

3 hours

2 hours

1½ hours

1 Teams arrive
Players make their way
to the ground up to three
hours before kick-off.
The away team arrives
on their team bus.

2 Team announcement
Both managers reveal their
team's starting line-up and
the list of substitutes to
the press.

3 Focusing the mind
Players begin their mental
preparation. They each
have their own ritual for
staying relaxed and focused
right up to kick-off.

In 2012,
GSP Polet's Vuk
Bakic scored
**directly from
a kick-off** in a
Serbian league
match.

Countdown to kick-off

Before the **match** kicks off, the players
spend up to two hours preparing for
the **physical** and **mental** challenges
of the game ahead.

15 mins

15 mins

5 mins

4 Warm-up
Players take part in low-level exercise drills to warm up their key muscle groups.

5 Team talk
The team gathers in the changing room for a final pep talk. The referee asks the teams to line up in the tunnel five minutes before kick-off.

6 Sporting gesture
The two teams run onto the pitch and shake hands. The players then take their position on the pitch.

7 Kick-off
A coin-toss decides which team kicks off from the centre circle. The referee blows the whistle and the match gets underway.

Caught offside

An **attacker** is in an **offside position** if he or she steps closer to the **opponent's goal** than any of the **defenders** before the ball is **kicked to the player**. The rule stops attackers from **hanging** near to the goal.

Although in an offside position, the player is not active in play and, therefore, isn't committing an offside infringement.

ACTIVE IN PLAY

The offside rule applies only when an attacker receives the ball in the opposition's half of the field. In addition, the player must be active in play, or be gaining an advantage by being in that position.

In this match scenario, the attacking player has passed the ball to a teammate who is offside. The team is immediately penalized and the referee awards the opponent an indirect free kick.

An attacker is **not offside** if the ball is **received** from a **corner, throw-in,** or **goal-kick.**

Player A stays onside, as he is level with the defender closest to the goal line.

2. **Player B** is offside. He is closer to the opposition goal than any of the defenders when he receives the pass and becomes active in play.

3. **The assistant referee** stands in line with the defender closest to the goal. The official raises the flag to signal that an attacking player is offside.

A

B

1. **The attacker** puts the team in an offside position by passing the ball to player B. The pass should have been made to player A.

The line of offside is based on the position of the defender who is closest to the team's goal line.

4. **The referee** spots the assistant referee's offside signal and stops play. The defending team will be awarded an indirect free kick.

FAST FACTS

Originally, the offside rule forced attackers to stay in front of two defenders. The rule was revised to a single defender in 1925, and led to a 36 per cent increase in the number of goals across the English leagues in the following season.

1924–25 season
4,700 goals

1925–26 season
6,373 goals

What is a foul?

The rules state that football must be played **fairly** and **safely**. It is the **referee's** job to call a **foul** if a player commits an **unfair act**, and to award the opposition a **free kick** – or a **penalty** if the foul occured in the penalty box.

FAST FACTS

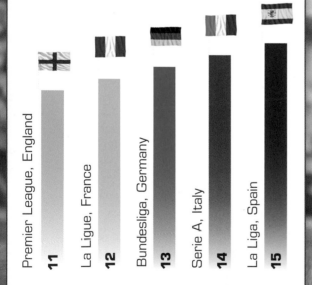

Premier League, England **11**

La Ligue, France **12**

Bundesliga, Germany **13**

Serie A, Italy **14**

La Liga, Spain **15**

The teams in Europe's top five leagues commit between 11 and 15 fouls per match. The English Premier League records the lowest number – this is perhaps because the referees are more lenient.

COMMON FOULS

A foul can be committed in a number of ways. Below are among the most common:

Handball
Deliberately using the hand or lower arm to control the ball.

Obstruction
Blocking an opponent without making any attempt to play the ball.

Tripping
Intentionally tripping up an opponent.

Holding
Pulling on an opponent's shirt to slow him down.

Dangerous play
Making a reckless tackle that endangers a player's safety.

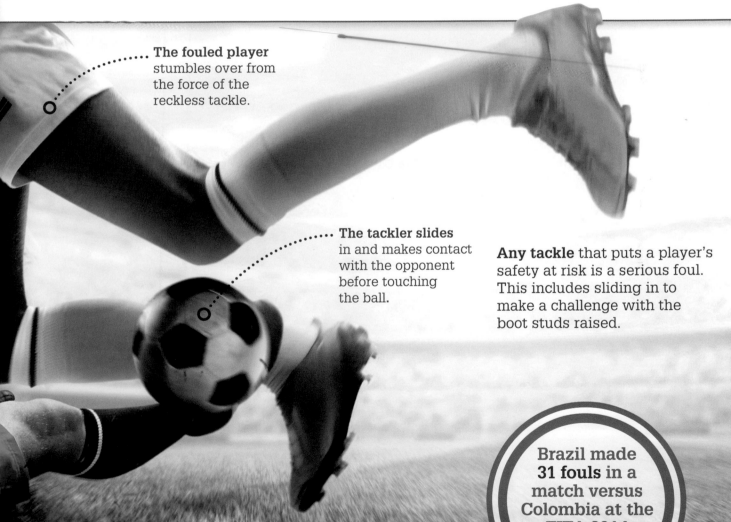

The fouled player stumbles over from the force of the reckless tackle.

The tackler slides in and makes contact with the opponent before touching the ball.

Any tackle that puts a player's safety at risk is a serious foul. This includes sliding in to make a challenge with the boot studs raised.

Brazil made **31 fouls** in a match versus Colombia at the FIFA 2014 World Cup!

Free kicks

A team wins a **free kick** whenever the opposition commits a **foul** outside their own penalty area. The free kick is taken from the **spot** where the offence occurred and, if it is close to the opponent's goal, can present a good **goal-scoring chance**.

If a team shoots a **free kick** into its **own goal,** the opposition is awarded a **corner.**

Curving shot

The goalkeeper guard the area around the post nearest to him.

TYPES OF FREE-KICK

Signal for a direct free kick.

Signal for an indirect free kick.

There are two types of free kick – direct and indirect. The referee awards a direct free-kick for a foul, whereas an indirect free kick results from a technical infringement. Direct free kicks can be shot straight into goal, but an indirect free kick must be touched by a teammate first.

In this direct free kick, the player has a shot on goal. It is up to him to decide where to direct the shot, and then either drill, curve, spin, or apply dip to the ball.

SHOOTING OPTIONS

Curving shot
The free-kick taker strikes across the ball with the side of the foot. This applies spin and makes the ball curve in the air.

Dipping shot
In this type of free kick, the player puts top spin on the ball by striking it with the laces and then shortening the follow-through.

Through the wall
The player shoots the ball low and fast underneath the wall. This may catch any defenders, who leap up expecting an aerial shot, off-guard.

The defensive wall is made up of several players who stand in a line to guard the goal. They must be at least 9 m (10 yd) away from the ball.

Dipping shot

Curving shot

Through the wall

The free-kick taker is a specialist who can direct the shot with pace and accuracy.

The top left-hand corner of the goal is the natural side for the right-footed player to aim.

The inner arc (red) represents the goalkeeper's "diving envelope". Any shots placed in this area are within his reach and will be saved if he dives the right way.

The average speed of a penalty is 112 km/h (70 mph).

SENSATIONAL SHOOTOUT

The 1994 FIFA World Cup final was the first to be decided by a penalty shootout. Brazil won the match after Italy's star player, Roberto Baggio, ballooned the decisive penalty over the bar.

Goalkeepers will choose the right way to dive 70 per cent of the time, according to statistics.

The orange arc represents a zone in which the goalkeeper can still reach the ball by diving. Any shots placed here can still be saved.

Penalties placed in the top corners are unsaveable, even by world-class goalkeepers. However, they carry a higher risk of missing the target.

That gives a goalkeeper **only 700 milliseconds** to save it.

A penalty **shootout** in the 2005 Namibian Cup final ended 17–16.

Deciding where to place the ball when taking a penalty depends on a number of factors. Are you right- or left-footed? Is the goalkeeper right- or left-handed? How much of a risk are you prepared to take?

Taking penalties

The penalty kick is one of the most dramatic moments in a football match. A **single kick** from the **penalty spot** can determine which team **wins or loses** the match, or even the entire league.

Corners

A team wins a **corner** whenever the ball **crosses the byline** after touching an opposition player. A corner presents a chance to play the ball into a **good attacking position**.

From a corner, the ball can be played anywhere on the pitch, but the corner taker typically chooses either the far post, the near post, the penalty spot, or to the nearest teammate. The aim is to create the best opportunity to score.

The corner taker is the team's dead-ball specialist, who is skilled at delivering the ball with great accuracy.

Far-post corner

Near-post corner

Penalty-spot corner

The ball must be placed on or behind the corner arc marking.

FAST FACTS

From the 13,000 corners taken in the English Premier League over two seasons (2011–13), 2,150 led to a shot, of which only 370 resulted in a goal – equating to about three per cent.

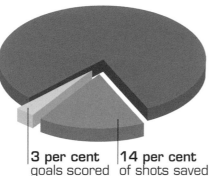

83 per cent of corners cleared

3 per cent goals scored

14 per cent of shots saved

TYPES OF CORNER

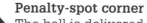

Far-post corner
The ball is played into the area around the goal post that is furthest away from the corner-taker.

Near-post corner
The ball is kicked to a teammate positioned at the post closest to the corner flag, who uses the head to flick the ball across goal into a striker's path.

Penalty-spot corner
The ball is delivered to an unmarked attacker in the penalty area who is in a position to shoot.

Short corner
The ball is passed to the nearest teammate who is in a better position to cross the ball into the penalty area.

Players aiming to score from a corner move around in the penalty area to get away from their marker.

One goal was scored from every 70 corners taken at the 2010 FIFA World Cup.

Short corner

The card system

If a player commits a **serious foul**, the referee shows the **offender** a card. A **yellow card** is a final warning, whereas a player shown a **red card** must leave the pitch right away.

English referee **Ken Aston** invented the card system after the 1966 FIFA World Cup.

The referee points to the dressing room immediately after showing the offender a red card. According to the Laws of the Game, the sent-off player cannot remain on – or anywhere around – the field of play.

The red and yellow cards are sometimes kept in different pockets, so the referee avoids pulling out the wrong card in the heat of the moment.

REFEREE'S NOTEBOOK

The referee uses a notebook to record key facts and incidents that occur in the match. This includes goal times, details of any substitutions made, and the names of players who have received a red or yellow card.

The sent-off player cannot be replaced. The team must play the rest of the match with one less player.

📊 FAST FACTS

A player receives a yellow card for offences such as those listed opposite. A red card is shown for very serious offences, such as those listed below.

Yellow card offences

- Rough tackling
- Arguing with the referee
- Holding an opponent
- Blocking the goalkeeper
- Deliberate time-wasting
- Refusing to move the proper distance from a free kick
- Deliberate handball
- Unsporting behaviour

Red card offences

- Dangerous tackling
- Violent conduct
- Using bad language
- Spitting at an opponent or any other person
- Denying the opposition a goal-scoring chance with a deliberate foul
- Receiving a second yellow card

Goal-line **technology**

Goal-line technology (GLT) is a **computerized system** introduced in 2012 to help officials in situations when it is difficult to tell whether the **ball has crossed the goal line** for a goal.

HOW IT WORKS:

1 Seven fast-frame cameras located above and around each goal track the ball's movement in the goal area.

2 The cameras send the information to a computer, which analyses whether the ball has crossed the goal line.

Goal-line technology is able to relay the result to the referee within a second of the incident taking place, which means there is no delay to the game.

COSTLY ERRORS

Following several refereeing errors at the 2010 FIFA World Cup — including a disallowed England goal in their 4—1 defeat to Germany (above) — FIFA decided to bring in goal-line technology.

The GLT system only **relays information** to the match officials.

FAST FACTS

A goal is awarded when the officials are sure that every part of the ball has crossed the goal line. Goal-line technology is highly accurate, with a margin of error of only 3 mm (0.12 in).

Goal line

Pitch

Goal

Goal line

Pitch

No Goal

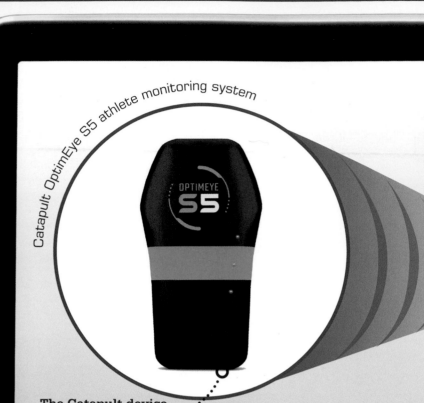

Catapult OptimEye S5 athlete monitoring system

OPTIMEYE S5

The Catapult device can analyse 1,000 items of data every second.

Tracking players

Many players wear a **tracking device** under their shirt. This provides **crucial information** about the player's **physical performance**.

The tracking device is placed between a player's shoulders. It gathers huge amounts of information, which can be analysed both during and after the match.

PRECISION PASSING

Every pass a player makes in a match is also recorded. Blue arrows are successful passes; red arrows are unsuccessful ones.

Data recieved

Heart-rate
A programme analyses a player's heart-rate during a match. Using this data, analysts can tell when players start to tire.

Number of sprints
The number of sprints a player makes in a game is tracked. A drop in number may indicate player fatigue or injury.

Metres per minute
Logging the amount of ground a player covers every minute reveals a player's overall fitness or stamina.

Total distance covered
The device also tracks the total amount of ground a player covers during the course of a match.

High-speed running
Analysts can tell the total distance a player has sprinted in a match. The higher the number, the fitter the player.

Acceleration
The device measures the total number of accelerations a player makes in a match, how long they last, and how much ground is covered.

Dynamic stress load
By tracking a player's movement the device calculates how hard the player is working throughout the match.

Deceleration
The total number of times a player slows down in a match is logged, and how much ground is covered.

Extra time

Gerardo Bedoya

has received **more red cards** than any other player in professional football. Capped **49 times** for Colombia, the defensive midfielder picked up **46 red cards** in a **20-year career** between 1995 and 2015.

BEDOYA
46

Red cards only became **compulsory** in **every** football game in **1982.**

The record for the *fastest dismissal* in a professional match is held by Bologna's **Giuseppe Lorenzo**. He was sent off after 10 seconds in an Italian Serie A match against Parma in 1990 for hitting an opponent.

00:10

Team shirt sales
Manchester United sell more replica shirts per year than any other club in world football.

1 Manchester United
1,750,000

2 Real Madrid
1,650,000

3 Barcelona
1,278,000

4 Bayern Munich
1,200,000

5 Chelsea
899,000

Colombia's Marcos Coll **is the only player** to score **directly from a corner** in a *FIFA World Cup match*. He scored the wonder goal against the *Soviet Union* at the **1962** tournament in Chile.

The longest

penalty shootout of all time in professional football occurred in a match between KK Palace and Civics in the Namibian Cup final in 2005. Forty-eight spot-kicks were taken before KK Palace finally triumphed 17–16.

On **wet**, *rainy days*, **old** leather footballs **could often double** in weight. **By the** *end of a match* **the ball could weigh as much as** **1 kg** **(2.2 lb).**

Shirt sponsorship

Shirt sponsorship has become a major source of revenue for clubs around the world, but the amount of money raised in this way varies from league to league. England's Premier League leads the way.

£226 million

£101 million

£82 million

£70 million

£61 million

| Premier League **England** | Bundesliga **Germany** | La Liga **Spain** | Ligue 1 **France** | Serie A **Italy** |

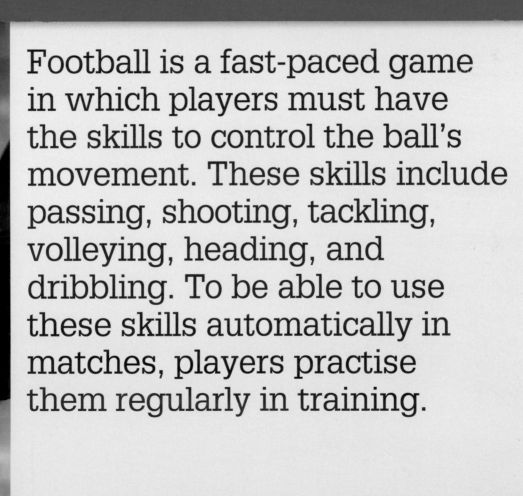

Individual skills

Football is a fast-paced game in which players must have the skills to control the ball's movement. These skills include passing, shooting, tackling, volleying, heading, and dribbling. To be able to use these skills automatically in matches, players practise them regularly in training.

Ball control

Any player who receives the ball must be able to bring it **under control** right away. The **quicker** the player can do this, the more **time and space** there will be to decide the next move.

1. Chest trap
Lean back and cushion the ball with the chest. The key is to slow the ball's speed at the point of contact.

2. Balance
Use the arms for balance and also to shield the ball from any opponents.

3. Ball position
As the ball drops to the ground in front of you, get ready to make a pass or run with the ball.

The quality of the "first touch" determines how quickly a player can control the ball. The best players can put the ball exactly where they want it with a single touch.

Professional players use an **average of two touches per possession.**

SKILL DRILL

In tight situations, use the top of the foot to control a ball that arrives at shin height, so you can make a pass or start a dribble.

Closely watch the ball as it comes to your foot

Relax the foot as the ball lands on it

Passing

Passing is the most **efficient way of moving the ball** towards the opponent's goal. Skilled players are able to make passes accurately along the **ground**, in the **air**, and over a **range of distances**.

The short pass is where the passer plays the ball to a nearby teammate. It is the most accurate form of passing.

The passing player strikes the ball with the side of his foot to make a short pass, the laces of the boot for a long pass, and the outside of the foot for a wide, diagonal pass.

SKILL DRILL

A short pass is a controlled pass made with the side of the foot. In this form of passing, the ball is kicked to a teammate along the ground and moves at a relatively slow speed.

1. Point the standing foot in the direction you want the ball to travel and strike the ball with the side of the foot.

Keep ankle locked at the point of contact

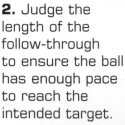

2. Judge the length of the follow-through to ensure the ball has enough pace to reach the intended target.

Sweep the striking foot across the ball

The player making the pass must be able to control the ball's speed and direction so that it reaches the intended teammate without being blocked by an opponent.

The long ball is played over a large distance towards the opponent's goal, in the hope that a teammate receives the ball and starts an attack.

The wide, diagonal pass is a long-range pass, normally made from inside the player's own half to a teammate near the touchline.

A long ball describes any pass that is longer than 32 m (35 yd).

TIKI-TAKA

Tiki-taka is a style of play in which a team passes and moves at high speed, denying the opposition possession of the ball. The style was introduced in the mid-2000s by Spanish club Barcelona, who won the Champions League trophy three times between 2008 and 2015.

Dribbling

The ability to move the ball past opposing players in tight spaces is known as **dribbling**. Good dribblers have **quick feet**, **great balance**, and create more goal-scoring chances.

The best dribblers keep the ball close to their feet. They move the ball using the inside and outside of both feet, as they twist and turn their way past defenders.

A player **dribbles** the ball an average distance of **191 m (208 yd)** in a match.

DRIBBLING DYNAMO

During the 1986 FIFA World Cup quarter-final match against England, Argentina's star player Diego Maradona dribbled past five English players to score one of the most memorable goals in FIFA World Cup history.

1. Look ahead
Assess the situation in front as you move forwards with the ball.

2. Shoulder feint
Drop the shoulder as though you are about to move in one direction, but take the ball the opposite way.

SKILL DRILL

The step over is a trick used to fool an opponent into thinking you're about to make a pass when the real aim is to dribble past them.

Drop shoulder

1. Approach the ball as if you are about to pass it with the outside of the foot.

Place weight on the non-kicking foot

Look straight ahead

Swivel the foot around the ball

2. Instead of passing, move the foot around the ball and then dribble in the opposite direction.

3. Beat the opponent
Use the outside of your foot to move the ball away from the challenger. Keep the ball close to your feet.

Shooting

If you want to be the team's **star goal scorer**, you will need **accurate shooting** skills. There are many shot types, but the most spectacular is the **power shot**, where a player **strikes the ball hard**, and hopes the **ball's speed** and direction will take it past the goalkeeper.

1. Ball-watching
Keep your eyes focused on the part of the ball you want to strike.

2. Body position
Keep your upper body over the ball during the shot so the ball stays low.

Fewer than **three out of every 20** goal-scoring attempts result in a goal.

SKILL DRILL

To make the ball curve or dip in the air, strike it in the area shown below with the highlighted part of the boot.

Inswinging shot – the ball will spin anti-clockwise and curve to the left.

Outswinging shot – the ball will spin clockwise and curve to the right.

When taking a power shot, aim to kick the ball either side of the goalkeeper. The hardest places for the keeper to reach are the four corners of the net.

5. Impact
Make firm contact with the bottom right part of the ball and follow through with the kicking leg.

3. Standing leg
Line up the non-kicking foot alongside the ball with the toe pointing in the direction you want to aim the shot.

4. Striking leg
Sweep the shooting leg smoothly and strike the ball with the instep for an inswinging shot.

GOAL MACHINE

Brazilian legend Pelé was among the finest goalscorers ever. In a glittering career that spanned 22 years (1955–77), he played 1,363 games and scored an amazing 1,281 goals.

Volleying

Striking the ball while it is in mid-air is known as volleying. Watching a player volley the ball into the **back of the net** is one of the most **stunning sights** in football.

3. Impact
Strike the ball firmly with the top of the boot.

4. Leg position
Keep the striking leg parallel to the ground during the follow through.

LONGEST VOLLEY

During a German league match in 2014, SC Paderborn's player Moritz Stoppelkamp volleyed the ball 82 m (90 yards) into an empty net to score the longest volleyed goal ever.

1. Head and body
Keep your head still and watch the ball closely throughout.

The scissor kick is a way of volleying a ball at waist height. Watch the ball's flight so you can time your leap correctly. While airborne, keep your legs apart like open scissors, then snap the kicking leg forward and strike the ball with power.

SKILL DRILL

The bicycle kick is an overhead volley where you kick the ball in the opposite direction to that in which you are facing.

Leap

1. Raise the non-kicking foot and leap into the air using the other foot.

Sweep

2. Once airborne, sweep the striking leg towards the ball.

Strike

3. Kick the ball over your head, and as you land use the hand to cushion the impact.

2. Hip movement
Swivel the hips quickly towards the ball to generate maximum power.

Striking the ball **on the bounce** or a **split-second** after is known as a **half-volley.**

Heading

Heading the ball is a vital skill for both **attackers** and **defenders**. Players who are expert headers **score more goals**, defend better, and win more battles for **possession**.

Giant leap
Time your jump correctly so that you meet the ball before any opposition players.

A HEAD FOR GOAL

At the 2002 FIFA World Cup tournament, German striker Miroslav Klose scored five goals in total — all of them were headers.

Firm contact
Use the forehead. This provides the most accuracy and power.

Pull up
Use your arms to pull yourself as high into the air as possible.

SKILL DRILL

When making a defensive header, the main aim is to knock the ball as far away as possible from the attacking player.

Use your forehead

Leap up to meet the ball

For a power header, the player leaps in the air and uses the neck muscles to sling his forehead to make contact with the ball.

Some players are able to leap 2.4 m (8 ft) to head the ball.

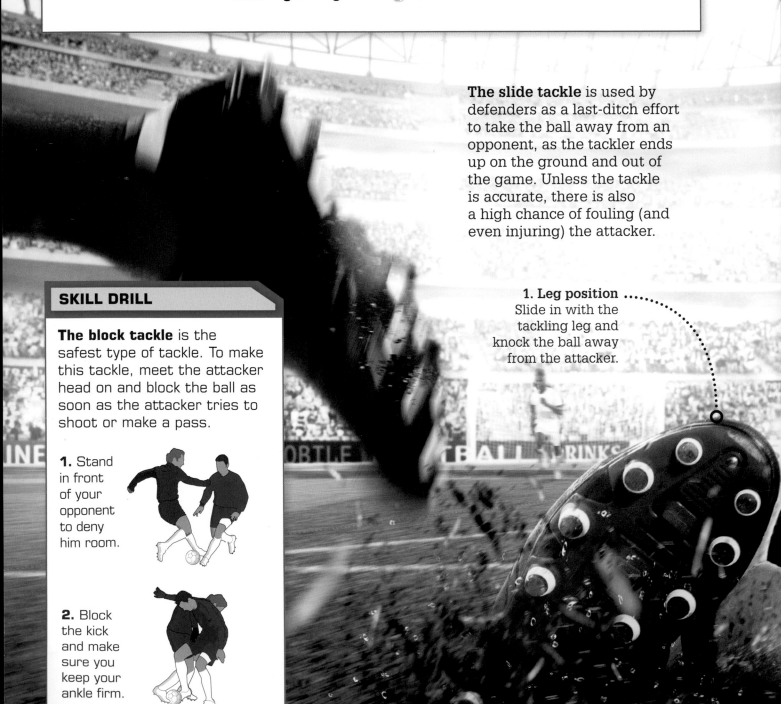

FAST FACTS

The chart opposite shows the number of different types of challenge a defender typically makes during the course of a match.

Tackle ⚽⚽⚽ 3
Header challenge ⚽ 1
Pressing opponent ⚽ 1
Blocking a shot or pass ⚽⚽⚽⚽⚽⚽⚽⚽⚽⚽⚽⚽⚽⚽⚽⚽⚽⚽ 19
Clearing a long ball ⚽ 1

The slide tackle is used by defenders as a last-ditch effort to take the ball away from an opponent, as the tackler ends up on the ground and out of the game. Unless the tackle is accurate, there is also a high chance of fouling (and even injuring) the attacker.

1. Leg position
Slide in with the tackling leg and knock the ball away from the attacker.

SKILL DRILL

The block tackle is the safest type of tackle. To make this tackle, meet the attacker head on and block the ball as soon as the attacker tries to shoot or make a pass.

1. Stand in front of your opponent to deny him room.

2. Block the kick and make sure you keep your ankle firm.

Tackling

A tackle is made to **take the ball away from an opponent**. The player must know how and when to make the tackle, so the **ball is won cleanly** without fouling or injuring the opponent.

The world's top defenders make about **five tackles in a match.**

3. Perfect timing
Watch the ball closely to make sure you take it cleanly from the opponent.

2. Support
Use the arms to support the body on the ground.

Extra time

Belgian goalkeeper **Kristof von Hout** is officially the world's tallest-ever player, measuring **2.08 m** (6.8 ft). Brazilian midfielder **Elton Gomes** is the **shortest,** standing at **1.54 m** (5.05 ft).

Across Europe's five major leagues, *the* **passing accuracy** averages out to **76.1 per cent** per match. Below are the individual percentages for each of the five leagues.

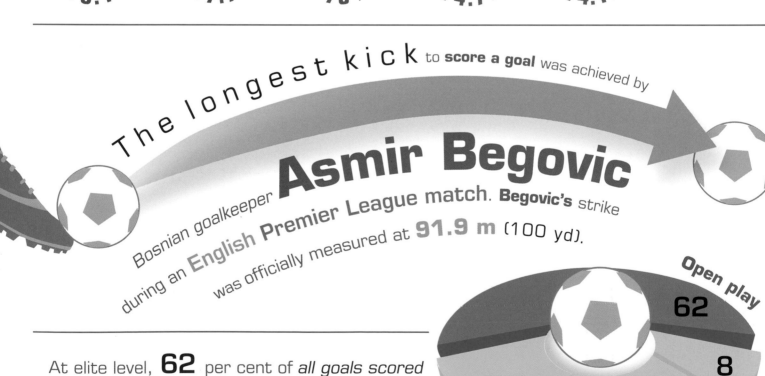

ITALY
Serie A
78.1%

GERMANY
Bundesliga
77.7%

FRANCE
Ligue 1
76%

SPAIN
La Liga
74.7%

ENGLAND
Premier League
74.1%

The longest kick to **score a goal** was achieved by

Asmir Begovic

Bosnian goalkeeper, during an **English Premier League** match. **Begovic's** strike was officially measured at **91.9 m** (100 yd).

At elite level, **62** per cent of *all goals scored* are from **open play. Free-kicks** and **corners** account for **30** per cent, and penalties make up **8** per cent.

Open play **62**

8

30

Penalties

Free-kicks and corners

A goal in every minute!

Star strikers Cristiano Ronaldo and **Zlatan Ibrahimovic** have **both** scored in **each minute**, from the **1st** to the **90th**, in competitive football.

The world record for the **longest headed goal** is *58 m (63.4 yd)*, scored by Odd's BK's **Joan Samuelsen** in 2011 against Tromsø in the **Norwegian Eliteserien** league.

The **best way** to spend the 15-minute half-time interval is to *rest* for the first **7.5 minutes** and then use the **other half** to do *light activity* to warm up the **muscles**.

Borussia Dortmund's Pierre-Emerick Aubameyang is the world's fastest player. He is said to have run **30 m (40 yd)** in a staggering **3.7 seconds** during training!

The most goals scored by a **single player** in a FIFA *World Cup finals tournament* was **13** by France's **Just Fontaine** in 1958.

A team game

Football is a team game of 11 players, who must work together to beat the opposition. The manager helps them to achieve this by making sure they practise hard on the training ground, by picking a formation to suit the players' strengths, and by ensuring the 11 players know their roles.

Goalkeeping

As the team's last line of defence, the goalkeeper has to be **quick** and good at **leaping**, **catching**, and **kicking**. This key player is allowed to **handle** the ball inside the team's **penalty area**, but nowhere else on the pitch.

HIGH ACHIEVER

Spanish goalkeeper Iker Casillas is one of the most successful goalkeepers of all time. He won five league titles, four Spanish Cups, two Champions League trophies, the Copa del Rey, and the UEFA Super Cup with Real Madrid between 1999 and 2015.

Pay close attention to the game, anticipate any dangers, and be ready to stop any shots.

Stay on your toes at all times, so you can leap in either direction to make a save.

Reach the ball with an outstretched hand and push it out of play.

The goalkeeper must always be ready to make a diving save, as skillful attackers tend to direct their shots into the corners of the goal.

Keep the wrist locked to keep the ball from slipping through the hands.

USA keeper Tim Howard **made 15 saves v Belgium at the 2014 FIFA World Cup.**

MARSHALLING THE DEFENCE

The goalkeeper is not just a shot-stopper, but also the leader in defence. It is the goalkeeper's job to organize the defenders so they can deal with any threats to goal. When defending free kicks, the goalkeeper forms the defensive wall by telling the defenders where to stand.

Full-back
Full-backs operate on either side of the pitch and defend the touchline. When one full-back goes on a forward run, the other will move across to support the centre halves.

Wing-back
Two wing-backs operate on either side of the pitch, but slightly up the field compared to the full-back. Wing-backs are responsible for both attacking and defending along the touchline.

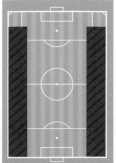

MATCH STATS
Distance: 10.0 km (6.2 miles)
Tackles: 2.0
Passes: 41.2
Clearances: 3.2

ATTACK

DEFENCE

DEFENCE

DEFENCE

DEFENCE

DEFENCE

ATTACK

MATCH STATS
Distance: 9.5 km (5.9 miles)
Tackles: 1.7
Passes: 41.9
Clearances: 5.9

DEFENCE

DEFENCE

DEFENCE

DEFENCE

DEFENCE

The sweeper used to be an important position in the past, but is rarely seen in the modern game. Not a single team used one at the 2014 FIFA World Cup.

Centre-back
A team usually places two centre-backs in front of the goalkeeper. They mark the opposition's most advanced forwards, and their main role is to clear the ball from the penalty area.

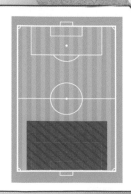

Sweeper
The sweeper is usually placed behind the centre halves. The player has no marking duties, so may move forwards during an attack. The use of a sweeper has fallen out of fashion in recent times.

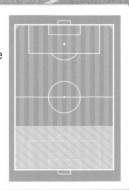

Dutch centre-back Ronald Koeman scored **253 goals** in his career – a record for a defender.

THE GREAT DEFENDER

A FIFA World Cup winner with West Germany in 1974, Franz Beckenbauer is considered one of the greatest defenders in football history. He redefined the role of a sweeper, from simply being a defensive stopper to becoming a team's creative attacking force.

ATTACK

MATCH STATS
Distance: 10.6 km (6.6 miles)
Tackles: 1.5
Passes: 34.8
Dribbles: 2.1

ATTACK

ATTACK

ATTACK

Solid defending

A defender's main job is **to stop the opponent from scoring a goal**. There are **four types** of defender: full-back, wing-back, centre-back, and sweeper (also known as a "libero").

Defenders must operate as a unit, but each has a different role to play. Full-backs make the most tackles, centre-backs execute the most clearances, while wing-backs have to run the furthest.

Defensive midfielder
This player's role is to stop an opponent's attack, and to cover in defence if one of his team's defenders joins an attack. Defensive midfielders will rarely advance into the opponent's half.

Central midfielder
In attack, central midfielders pass the ball and look to join the forwards. In defence, they drop back to help the defenders stop an opponent's attack.

MATCH STATS
Distance: 8.9 km
(5.5 miles)
Tackles: 5.5
Passes: 48.6
Dribbles: 0.9

Barcelona's **Xavi made a world record 125 passes** against Espanyol in 2014–15.

MATCH STATS
Distance: 10.3 km
(6.4 miles)
Tackles: 2.4
Passes: 47.3
Dribbles: 1.2

MATCH STATS
Distance: 9.1 km
(5.7 miles)
Tackles: 2.1
Passes: 43.0
Dribbles: 1.6

Midfield magic

Midfielders **break up** an opponent's play and **set in motion** their own team's attack. There are **four types of midfielder**: defensive midfielder, central midfielder, wide midfielder, and attacking midfielder.

Wide midfielder
A wide midfielder takes up a position close to the touchline. In attack, their main role is to provide crosses into the opponent's penalty area. In defence, they must drop back to provide extra cover.

Attacking midfielder
The attacking midfielder is the creative force of a team and a link between the midfield and a striker. Attacking midfielders only have a limited defensive role and rarely drop back in their own half.

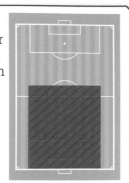

Midfielders have a crucial role to play in both defence and attack, with each type of player having to perform different tasks. Defensive midfielders average the most tackles per game, while central midfielders run the furthest. The number of midfield players a team fields depends on its formation.

DEFENCE

ATTACK

ATTACK

ATTACK

ATTACK

ATTACK

MATCH STATS
Distance: 10.1 km (6.3 miles)
Tackles: 1.7
Passes: 39.5
Dribbles: 1.3

MIDFIELD MASTER

Johan Cruyff was the best midfielder of his generation. During his 20-year career, he won eight Dutch league titles, one Spanish league title, and led the Netherlands to the FIFA World Cup final in 1974.

Flying forwards

Forwards are the players who are positioned **closest to an opponent's goal**. Their main job is to **score goals**, and they are often a team's most-celebrated, and expensive, players.

DEFENCE

ATTACK

DEFENCE

Forwards have to be fast. Some can run as fast as **9.7 m (10.6 yd) per second.**

MATCH STATS
Distance: 9.4 km (5.8 miles)
Tackles: 0.9
Passes: 28.5
Shots: 1.5

No.10/Second striker
The No.10 (also known as the second striker), plays in the space between an opponent's defence and midfield, commonly known as "the hole". From there, they will set up attacks or shoot for goal.

Winger
Part of an attacking formation, a winger is responsible for attacking down the edges of the pitch and for sending crosses into the penalty box. Wingers have limited defensive duties.

Centre forward
A centre forward's main job is to score goals and so they spend most of their time operating in an area in front of the opponent's goal. From here, they are in the best position to receive balls, turn, and score.

TOP STRIKE PARTNERSHIP

Two of the greatest forwards the game has ever seen, Alfredo Di Stéfano (left) and Ferenc Puskás combined with devastating effect for Real Madrid. Together, they propelled the Spanish giants to four consecutive league titles (1961–64) and two European Cups (1959 and 1960), and scored a staggering 258 goals in 182 league games.

ATTACK

ATTACK

ATTACK

MATCH STATS
Distance: 8.9 km (5.5 miles)
Tackles: 0.4
Passes: 18.3
Shots: 2.1

MATCH STATS
Distance: 9.3 km (5.8 miles)
Tackles: 1.0
Passes: 25.7
Shots: 1.7

DEFENCE

Forwards have many different roles. Centre forwards average the most shots per game. No.10s and wingers have to create goal-scoring opportunities for the centre forward.

Formations

A formation is the **way a team lines up on the pitch**. It is normally **described using a string of numbers**, which represent the number of players in each area of the pitch.

AC Milan won **the Champions League in 1989 and 1990 using** a 4-4-2.

4-4-2

The classic 4-4-2 formation has two lines of four in defence and midfield, with two forwards.

Two wide midfielders provide crosses for the two forwards in attack. They must also drop back to help out in defence.

Full-backs have a vital role to play in defence, but will often be used as extra attackers.

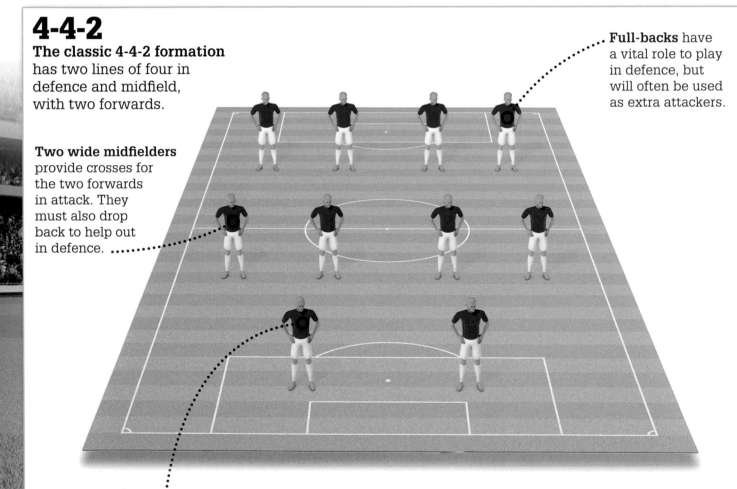

Forwards can advance to the opponent's goal without having to wait for support from the midfield.

✔ Advantages

- Two lines of four provide greater defensive cover.
- A pair of strikers creates a constant attacking threat.
- Full-backs provide extra width to stretch an opponent's defence.

✗ Disadvantages

- With only two central midfielders, a team can easily be outnumbered in midfield.
- Opponent can exploit the space between defence and midfield – called "the hole".
- This system places great pressure on midfielders both to attack and defend.

4-2-3-1

The dominant formation since the 2000s, this is still the preferred system in much of Europe.

Four defenders create a solid line of defence. The full-backs are expected to advance to create width in attack.

Wide midfielders have a vital role to play both in attack and defence.

Defensive midfielders provide extra cover in defence.

The single striker relies on support from the three attacking midfielders.

✔ Advantages

- It is easy to pass the ball through midfield.
- This system makes it hard for teams to be overrun in midfield.
- Three attacking midfielders provide a greater number of attacking options.

✘ Disadvantages

- The single striker relies on support from attacking midfielders.
- Attacking midfielders have to work very hard to cover in both defence and attack.
- This system places great responsibility on the wide players to drop back to help out in defence.

Other modern formations

4-1-2-1-2
Also known as "The Diamond", this formation provides greater solidity in midfield. Full-backs can move forward to provide the width in attack.

4-3-2-1
Named the "Christmas Tree" after its pointed shape, this is a more attacking variation of the 4-3-3, with two players playing behind a single striker.

4-3-3
Three midfielders move across the pitch as a unit. Because it has more attackers, many teams adopt this system if they are chasing a game.

More formations

4-5-1

A packed midfield means this is the formation of choice for teams looking to avoid defeat in knockout competitions.

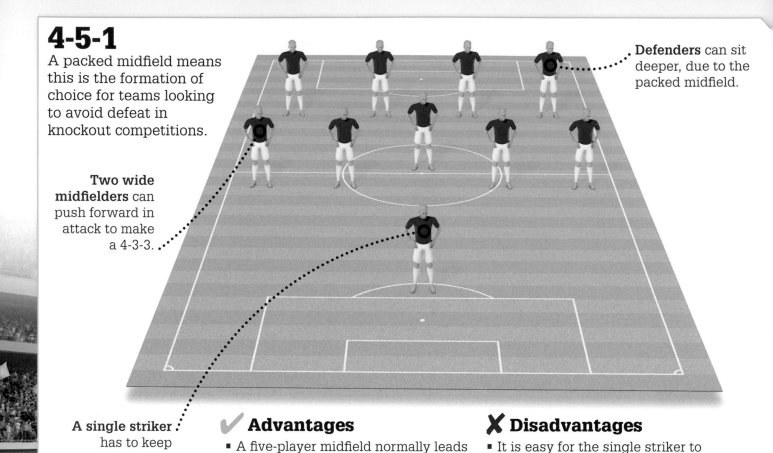

Defenders can sit deeper, due to the packed midfield.

Two wide midfielders can push forward in attack to make a 4-3-3.

A single striker has to keep possession of the ball in attack and wait for support.

✔ Advantages

- A five-player midfield normally leads to more possession of the ball.
- The formation is flexible. For example, it is easy to switch to a 4-3-3 in attack.
- This is a difficult formation for an opponent to break down.

✗ Disadvantages

- It is easy for the single striker to become isolated.
- The formation makes it difficult for teams to execute counter-attacks.
- Great pressure is placed on central midfielders to join the striker in attack.

BRAZIL BREAK THE MOULD

Developed to strengthen the defence without losing any numbers in attack, the 4-2-4 formation burst on to the scene when Brazil won the 1958 FIFA World Cup. In practice, it operates as a 4-3-3 in defence and as a 3-3-4 in attack.

Many think a **4-6-0** formation, with no striker, will be the **formation of the future**.

5-3-2/3-5-2

A pair of wing-backs provides extra options in both defence and attack, but they have to be incredibly fit to make the formation work.

The middle defender in the three-player defence must be good at passing, and is usually responsible for launching attacks.

Wing-backs provide width in attack and extra cover in defence.

Midfielders provide cover in defence and extra options in attack.

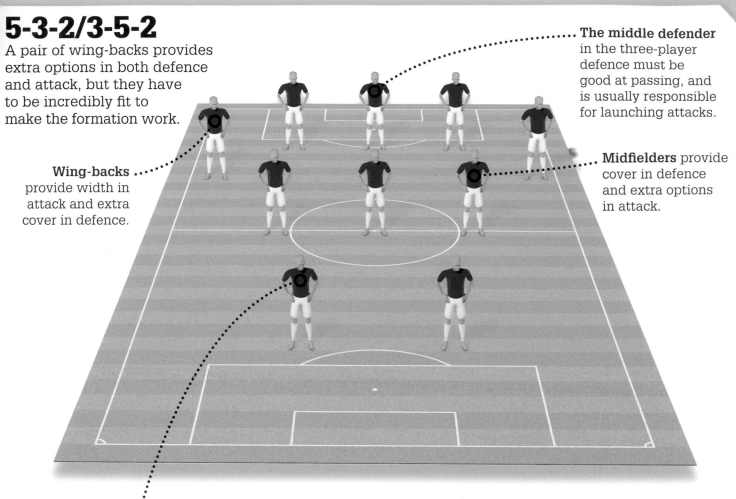

A pair of strikers can move forward to attack without having to wait for extra support from midfield.

✔ Advantages

- Three central defenders reduce the threat of an opponent's counter-attack.
- The defensive unit is usually helped by a deep-lying midfielder.
- Three midfielders and wing-backs provide a variety of attacking options.

✗ Disadvantages

- The back three must include at least one player who is good at passing the ball.
- Players require a superb sense of positioning to play in this formation.

Old formations

2-3-5
Known as "The Pyramid", this was the standard formation of the 1880s. It placed a huge emphasis on attacking.

3-2-2-3 (also known as WM)
First used in the 1920s, this formation reinforced the defence to counter the increased attacking threat that came about from a change in the offside rule.

Sweeper

1-4-3-2
Known as "catenaccio", this formation saw a sweeper (or "libero") positioned between the goalkeeper and the defence to add more defensive steel.

Set-pieces: attacking

Corners and **free kicks** are called **set-pieces**. They provide teams with the perfect opportunity to **execute set moves** they have spent **hours rehearsing** on the training ground.

The attacking side will often position a player in front of the near post. This player will look to flick the ball on with his head.

Where the corner taker delivers the ball will depend on the set move planned.

The players who are the best headers in the attacking team will line up near the edge of the penalty area and run towards goal as the corner is taken.

FAST FACTS

Although corners represent a good goal-scoring opportunity, not as many goals are scored from them as you might think.

5
Average number of corners a team wins in a match.

75
One in 75 corners taken leads directly to a goal.

45
One in 45 corners taken leads indirectly to a goal.

6%
Percentage of goals scored from corners at the 2010 FIFA World Cup.

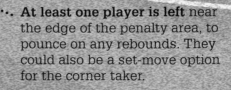

At least one player is left near the edge of the penalty area, to pounce on any rebounds. They could also be a set-move option for the corner taker.

Set piece: free kick

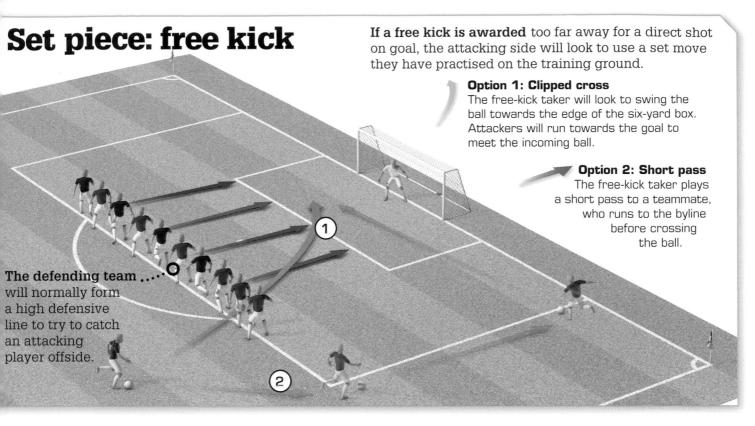

If a free kick is awarded too far away for a direct shot on goal, the attacking side will look to use a set move they have practised on the training ground.

Option 1: Clipped cross
The free-kick taker will look to swing the ball towards the edge of the six-yard box. Attackers will run towards the goal to meet the incoming ball.

Option 2: Short pass
The free-kick taker plays a short pass to a teammate, who runs to the byline before crossing the ball.

The defending team will normally form a high defensive line to try to catch an attacking player offside.

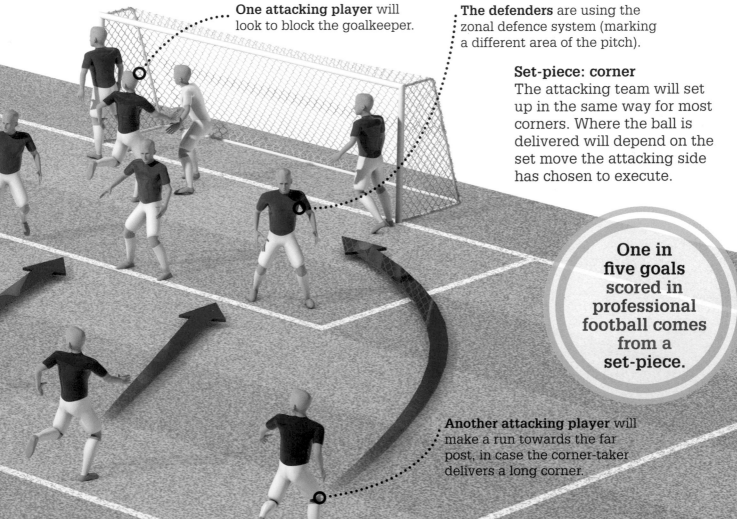

One attacking player will look to block the goalkeeper.

The defenders are using the zonal defence system (marking a different area of the pitch).

Set-piece: corner
The attacking team will set up in the same way for most corners. Where the ball is delivered will depend on the set move the attacking side has chosen to execute.

One in five goals scored in professional football comes from a set-piece.

Another attacking player will make a run towards the far post, in case the corner-taker delivers a long corner.

Set-pieces: defending

Because **set-pieces** offer such a good goal-scoring opportunity, it is **vital that a defence is organized** to deal with the impending threat.

Italian Serie A side Sassuolo **only conceded one goal** from a set-piece in 2014–15.

Teams use two main systems when they are defending corners: zonal marking or man-marking

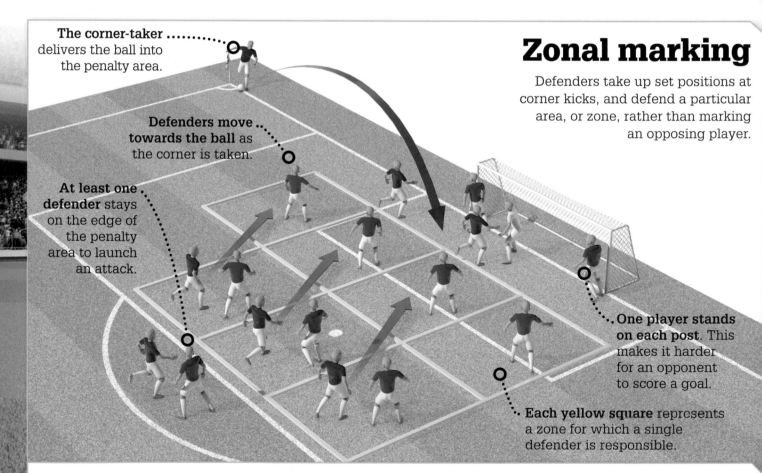

The corner-taker delivers the ball into the penalty area.

Defenders move towards the ball as the corner is taken.

At least one defender stays on the edge of the penalty area to launch an attack.

Zonal marking

Defenders take up set positions at corner kicks, and defend a particular area, or zone, rather than marking an opposing player.

One player stands on each post. This makes it harder for an opponent to score a goal.

Each yellow square represents a zone for which a single defender is responsible.

✔ Advantages
- This system leaves goalkeeper free to come and collect the ball, because the area around him/her is likely to be less congested.
- Defending becomes a team responsibility.

✘ Disadvantages
- It is easier for attackers to win a header, because, as they have a further distance to run towards the ball, they can arrive at it at greater speed and leap higher.

Defensive walls for free kicks

The goalkeeper decides how many players should be in a defensive wall. That number depends on where the free kick is taken from. Each segment in this illustration shows how many players would be in a wall if a free kick is taken inside it.

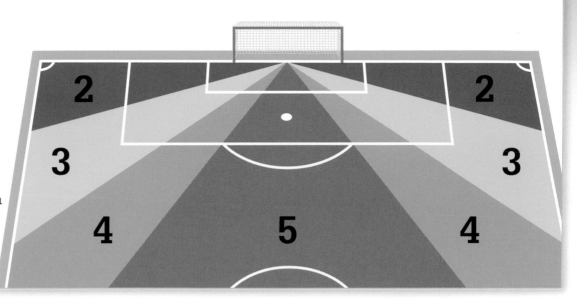

Man-marking

Each defender picks up an opposition player, and is responsible for staying with him until the ball has been cleared and the danger is over.

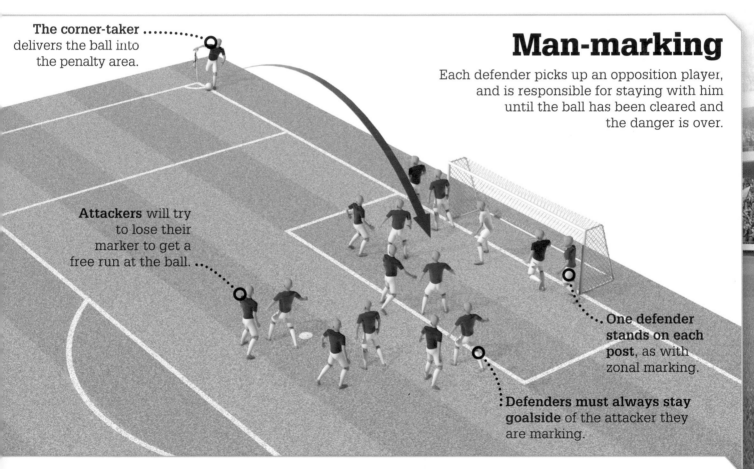

The corner-taker delivers the ball into the penalty area.

Attackers will try to lose their marker to get a free run at the ball.

One defender stands on each post, as with zonal marking.

Defenders must always stay goalside of the attacker they are marking.

✔ Advantages

- Defenders can get the same run at the ball as attackers.

✗ Disadvantages

- Defenders can get dragged around the penalty area by attackers.
- The system places great responsibility on the individual defender not to lose the attacker they are marking.
- The area around the goal mouth can become congested, making it difficult for the goalkeeper to come and claim the ball.

Football genius

Every team takes to the pitch with a **strategy** to help them win the match. This is devised by the **manager**, based on a **style of play** the team has developed over many years.

1930s

The passing method of play was introduced in 1870 by Scottish side Queen of the South. The team revolutionized the game from one that was solely based on dribbling.

1870s

Herbert Chapman founded the WM formation in the 1930s while managing English club Arsenal. The strategy focused on defence – previously the game was all about attacking.

Hungary scored a record **27 goals** at the **1954 FIFA World Cup.**

Helenio Herrera managed Italian side Inter Milan to European Cup glory in 1964 and 1965. Using a defensive style called catenaccio, the team won matches by scoring on the counter-attack.

1960s

The era of modern football has seen the emergence of many different strategies and playing styles. Here is a selection that have led to great success on the pitch.

Hungary played a unique formation in the 1950s, which saw the striker swap roles with midfielders, pulling opposition players out of position. The team won the Olympic gold medal in 1952.

1950s

2000s

The Netherlands team of the 1970s adopted a style of play known as Total Football, in which players swapped roles on the pitch. The team were FIFA World Cup finalists in 1974 and 1978.

Pep Guardiola's reign at Spanish club Barcelona saw the side using a possession-based style called Tiki-taka to win multiple trophies between 2008–2012.

Vicente del Bosque masterminded Spain's FIFA World Cup triumph in 2010. The team used a system called the False Nine, which features no recognized striker, but a trio of attacking midfielders instead.

2010

1970s

2010s

RINUS MICHELS

Rinus Michels is credited as inventing Total Football. In 1971, he led Dutch side Ajax to the first of three successive European Cup wins. He also introduced the style of play to Spanish side Barcelona and the Netherlands team, leading the Dutch to European Championship glory in 1988.

Jurgen Klopp led German club Borussia Dortmund to league titles in 2011 and 2012. He used a strategy called Gegenpressing, in which a team moves further up the pitch every time it loses possession to win back the ball as quickly as possible.

Extra time

The **average** number of **goals scored per game** across the top leagues in **China, England, France, Germany, Italy, Spain,** and the **USA** is **2.78**.

Spanish club **Barcelona** made a *record*

993 **passes** against German side **Borussia Mönchengladbach** in a 2011 **Champions League match. Barcelona won the game 4–0**.

During a **90-minute game** (excluding injury time), the **actual time the ball is in play** ranges between **60** and **65** **minutes**. At non-professional level, the figure is between **50** and **55** **minutes**.

The **most common scoreline** in football matches is 1–1, making up **11** per cent of all results. Here are the percentages of other common scorelines

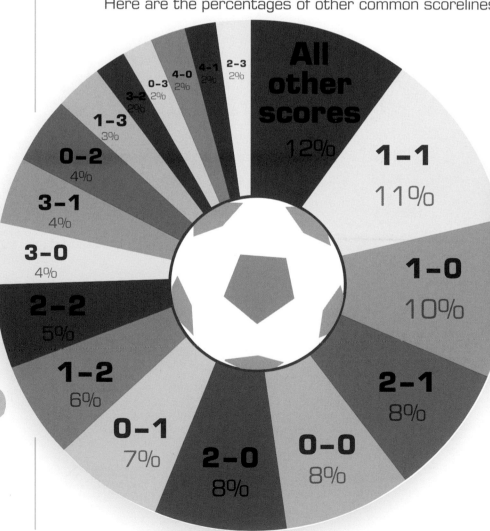

All other scores 12%

1–1 11%

1–0 10%

2–1 8%

0–0 8%

2–0 8%

0–1 7%

1–2 6%

2–2 5%

3–0 4%

3–1 4%

0–2 4%

1–3 3%

3–2 2%

0–3 2%

4–0 2%

4–1 2%

2–3 2%

A study of the English Premier League reveals **when goals** are **commonly scored** during a match.

0–15 minutes	**12.2% of goals**
16–30 minutes	**12.4% of goals**
31–45 minutes	**18.7% of goals**
46–60 minutes	**16.7% of goals**
61–75 minutes	**16.6% of goals**
76–90 minutes	**23.4% of goals**

In professional football, the **team that scores first** has only a **one in seven chance** of losing the match.

The longest-ever **undefeated run of matches** in top-level football are:

Celtic (Scotland) 1915–17

62 MATCHES

Union SG (Belgium) 1933–35

60 MATCHES

Benfica (Portugal) 1963–65

48 MATCHES

Dinamo Zagreb (Croatia) 1915–17

45 MATCHES

Juventus (Italy) 2011–12

43 MATCHES

On average, **9** out of every **100 shots** result in a **goal**. In contrast, **12** out of every **100 headers** on goal end up in the *back of the net*.

Dutch side Ajax won all **46 home games** for *two seasons in a row* (1971–72 and 1972–73), also picking up **four titles**: the **Dutch league title**, the **KNVB Cup**, the **European Cup**, and the **Intercontinental Cup**.

Club world

A football team is part of a much larger organization – the club, which has its own identity and tradition. Top clubs are run like businesses and employ hundreds of people. There are many different jobs to be done to keep a club running, from managing the team to selling tickets to fans and preparing the pitch for match day.

Running a club

A large football club **employs people** with many different skills to ensure it **succeds on the pitch** and as a **business.**

This diagram shows the different people who work at a football club, and explains what they do and how they work together to ensure the club runs smoothly.

English club **Notts County** is recognized as **the world's first** professional football club.

The directors are usually part owners of the club. They make the decisions about the club and its future plans.

BOARD OF DIRECTORS

The commerical director's role involves negotiating deals with sponsors and other businesses.

COMMERCIAL DIRECTOR

The chief executive officer (CEO) manages the day-to-day running of the whole club, and reports to the board of directors.

CEO

The manager is in charge of the first team. He or she controls training, picks the team, and sets the tactics for every match.

FIRST TEAM MANAGER

The financial director looks after the club's funds, and makes sure the club is making a profit.

FINANCIAL DIRECTOR

The technical director devises the coaching programmes and is also in charge of signing new players.

TECHNICAL DIRECTOR

medical care for the
first team squad.

CLUB DOCTOR

PHYSIO

The physio takes
care of injured players and
reports to the club doctor.

FIRST TEAM

ASSISTANT MANAGER

manager helps the
first team manager
prepare the team
for every match.

The team is picked
from a total squad
of 20–30 players,
who provide cover
for any injuries.

COACHES

Coaches are responsible
for the team's training. Each
coach specializes in a
different aspect of training.

SCOUTS

Scouts attend other
football matches on
behalf of the club
and look out for
talented players.

YOUTH FOOTBALL DEVELOPMENT MANAGER

**The youth development
manager** is in charge of
the local youth leagues.

SALES

The head of sales
oversees the
sale of tickets and
club merchandise.

LOCAL FOOTBALL DEVELOPMENT OFFICER

**The development
officer** organizes
and delivers a range
of football activities for
the local community.

The manager

Managers have to juggle **many tasks**. They are responsible for every aspect of **every team at a club**, from youth team to the first XI, and must also **speak to journalists**.

A manager's main task is to make sure the team wins as many games as possible. However, a manager's day does not end with the final whistle. He or she still has many other tasks to perform.

Guy Roux managed French club **Auxerre** for **44 years** (1961–2004).

In the spotlight

■ Dealing with the media.
■ Preparing programme notes.
■ Helping club sponsors.
■ Attending club events.
■ Appearing on the club's TV channel.

Team and players

- Deciding on formations.
- Selecting the team.
- Motivating the players.
- Giving team talks before and during the match.
- Making substitutions.

Behind the scenes

- Maintaining player discipline.
- Overseeing player development and promoting players.
- Setting coaching policy.

Running the club

- Buying and selling players.
- Appointing coaching staff.
- Overseeing coaching activities.
- Attending board meetings.
- Scouting for new players.

MANAGERIAL MERRY-GO-ROUND

England (Premier League)	11
Italy (Serie A)	21
Spain (La Liga)	16
France (Ligue 1)	11
Germany (Bundesliga)	11

The job of a top-flight football manager is among the least secure in the world. This chart shows the average number of managerial changes each year in Europe's top-five leagues.

The Allianz Arena is lit in **different colours** when the different home teams play.

📊 KEY

1 Team bus parking bay
2 Players' entrance
3 Away team changing room
4 Home team changing room
5 Warm-up room
6 Match officials' room
7 Press conference hall

Opened in 2005, the Allianz Arena in Germany can hold up to 75,000 fans, making it among the largest football stadiums in Europe. This is where club sides Bayern Munich and TSV 1860 Munich play their home matches.

Players' entrance

A separate entrance allows players to enter the stadium privately, and avoid the large crowd of fans in the ground.

The stadium

A team's stadium features a pitch surrounded by **thousands of seats** for the fans who come to watch the matches. It also includes all the **facilities** players need to prepare for a match.

Changing room

The changing room is where players change into their kit and gather for the manager's final team talk.

The tunnel

The players' tunnel leads on to the pitch. Players of both teams line up in the tunnel before the match.

A scout's job is to find talented new players. Larger clubs may have as many as 15 scouts.

Player scouted

Transfers

Professional football has two **transfer windows**: the first runs from July to September, and the second is in January. They are an exciting time for football fans, but **how do transfers actually work?**

Finding the right player is only the start of a long process. A club has to go through many stages before a player officially signs for them.

The bid

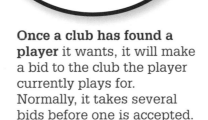

Agent talks

Once a club has found a player it wants, it will make a bid to the club the player currently plays for. Normally, it takes several bids before one is accepted.

After the bid has been accepted, a club starts contract talks with the player's agent. The two parties must agree on details such as wages and performance-related bonuses.

WORTH HIS WEIGHT IN GOLD

The first player who was literally worth his weight in gold was Bernabé Ferreyra. Argentine club River Plate paid £23,000 for his services in 1932, comfortably more money than his equivalent weight in gold at the time.

An agent's commission is usually 5 per cent of the transfer fee.

Once the player has passed the medical, the deal is officially done.

Done deal

inalizing contracts

The player and the buying club must agree on every detail in the contract. One Premier League player had a clause in his contract that prevented him from travelling to space!

The medical

Once the contract is finalized, a player has to go through a thorough medical examination to confirm fitness. This identifies any hidden injuries or weaknesses.

Training

Players mainly **practise** their **ball skills** during training, but also work on their **speed** and **agility**, **stamina**, **strength**, and **tactical awareness**.

Speed and agility

High-intensity exercises, such as sprints around obstacles, shuttle runs, hurdle hopping, and squat jumps all help to improve a player's speed and agility.

📊 FAST FACTS

Football 11–15 km (7–9.5 miles)

Rugby 6.5 –11 km (4–7 miles)

Hockey 6.5–8 km (4–5 miles)

Tennis 5–8 km (3–5 miles)

Basketball 3–5 km (2–3 miles)

American Football 2 km (1.25 miles)

Football players are exceptionally fit. They typically cover a distance of between 11–15 km (7–9.5 miles) during a 90-minute match.

Ball skills

Players regularly practise their ball skills. They also play training matches in which they work on set-pieces and different modes of attack and defence.

Professional players spend an average of **three hours a day** training.

DRINK ENOUGH WATER

During training, players shed between 1 and 1.5 kg (2.2–3.2 lbs) of weight through sweat loss. The amount can rise to 3 kg (6.5 lbs) during a match played on a hot day. To stay hydrated, experts recommend that players consume about 1.2–1.5 litres (40–50 fl oz) of fluid for each kilogram (2.2 lbs) of weight they lose.

Stamina

The team performs stamina-building exercises such as running and circuit drills. All players must be fit enough to play a full match without tiring.

Strength

Gym workouts are specially devised to develop players' leg muscles and overall body strength.

Tactical awareness

The coach works with the players to make sure they know their roles and can follow the game plan during the high-pressure situation of a match.

Injury time

Football is a physical game in which players have to **sprint, jump, twist, turn,** and **tackle.** These actions place huge stress on the **muscles, joints,** and **bones,** and can sometimes cause **injuries.**

Concussion
Head injury resulting from a collision with another player.

Shoulder dislocation
Dislodged shoulder bone caused by an awkward fall.

Professional players sustain an average of **two injuries** per season.

Back strain
Muscle sprain or tear from over-stretching the spine.

Broken finger
An injury suffered mostly by goalkeepers.

The red circles highlight the parts of the body that players are most likely to injure in a match. The number inside each circle refers to the number of injuries suffered in that area of the body out of every 100 injuries.

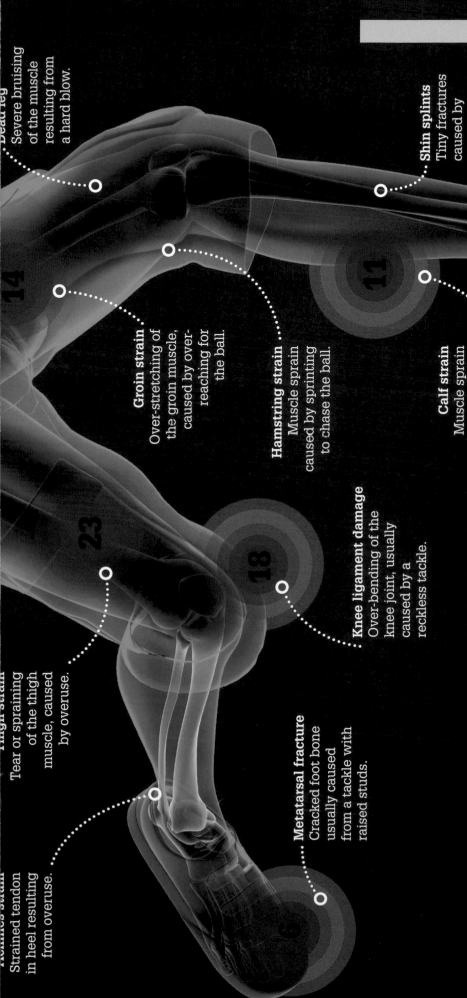

Dead leg
Severe bruising of the muscle resulting from a hard blow.

Shin splints
Tiny fractures caused by constant impact.

14

Groin strain
Over-stretching of the groin muscle, caused by over-reaching for the ball.

11

Hamstring strain
Muscle sprain caused by sprinting to chase the ball.

14

Calf strain
Muscle sprain or tear from over-stretching the lower leg.

Twisted ankle
Severe sprain caused by turning too rapidly or a bad tackle.

23

18

Knee ligament damage
Over-bending of the knee joint, usually caused by a reckless tackle.

Thigh strain
Tear or spraining of the thigh muscle, caused by overuse.

Achilles strain
Strained tendon in heel resulting from overuse.

Metatarsal fracture
Cracked foot bone usually caused from a tackle with raised studs.

The physio's role

Physios treat players who get injured during a match and help with their recovery afterwards. They also assess the fitness of players, and help devise individual training programmes to ensure a team's players stay fit throughout the season.

A player's week

Most professional footballers lead very **disciplined lives**. They follow a **strict routine** to ensure they are **fully prepared** for a **match**. This includes getting as much **rest** as possible between matches.

ICE BATHS

After every game, players take ice baths to treat muscle soreness. The cold makes the blood vessels tighten, draining out the blood. This allows oxygen-rich blood to get into the muscles, which speeds up recovery.

	Monday	Tuesday
MORNING	Aerobic training	Practice match
AFTERNOON	Individual ball skills	Physio sess
	Strength training	Medical assessmen fitness tes
EVENING	Free time	Free tim

Below is an example of a professional player's weekly timetable. It reveals just how much training is involved. Recovery time is equally important – players need about 8–10 hours of sleep a night.

Professional footballers spend about **15 hours a week training with the ball.**

	Thursday	Friday	Saturday	Sunday
...nesday ...ical ...aration	Recovery – light and low impact workout	Power and speed training session	Group ball skills	Recovery – light and low impact workout
...ching – ...s on ...bility	Post-match debrief led by the manager	Practice match	Travel to away match on team bus	Post-match debrief led by the manager
...p skills	Individual ball skills	Tactical preparation	AWAY MATCH K.O: 3.00pm	Physio session
...ME MATCH: ...: 7.45pm	Free time	Free time	Travel back from away match	Free time

The fans

True **football fans** are not just spectators, but keen participants who think of themselves as the team's **"twelfth" player**. They **chant**, **sing**, and voice their **opinions**, creating the **lively atmosphere** that spurs the team on.

Replica jerseys, **hats, and scarves** bearing the team's colours are worn to the match.

Eight out of 10 fans believe that their support helps the team to play better.

Fans revel in the loud and energetic atmosphere they create in the stadium. Some look forward to being around fellow fans as much as watching the game itself.

FAST FACTS

Football has a global fan base of about 3.5 billion people, which is more than any other sport in the world. About 64 per cent of these fans are male and 36 per cent are female.

3.5 billion

Football

2.5 billion

Cricket

2.2 billion

Basketball

2 billion

Tennis

1 billion
Volleyball

0.9 billion

Field hockey

Die-hard fans often use the melody of popular songs to make up catchy chants.

Some fans wave flags to show their support.

FAN POWER

The general trend across world football reveals that home sides win half of their matches and lose just one in four. This has much to do with the atmosphere home fans create, which helps give their side a mental advantage over the away team.

Extra time

The football clubs with the **highest number** of **fans** worldwide are:

2
Barcelona
(Spain)
290 million
fans

1
Manchester
United
(England)
670 million
fans

4
Chelsea
(England)
145 million
fans

3
Real Madrid
(Spain)
195 million
fans

5
Arsenal
(England)
125 million
fans

Europe's **longest-serving football managers** are:

5	**Vittori Pozzo:** 21 yrs (1929–48) at Italy (National team)	
4	**Alex Ferguson:** 27 yrs (1986–2013) at Manchester United (England)	
3	**Bill Struth:** 34 yrs (1921–1954) at Rangers (Scotland)	
2	**Willie Maley:** 43 yrs (1897–1940) at Celtic (Scotland)	
1	**Guy Roux:** 44 yrs (1961–2005) at Auxerre (France)	

How old are football fans?

The chart shows the **percentage** of all football fans in five different age groups.

16–24	25–34	35–44	45–54	55–64
20%	28%	20%	18%	13%

77 **per cent** of **European fans** have **travelled abroad** to watch a match. **England** is the most **popular country** for fans to visit to watch a football game, followed by **Spain**.

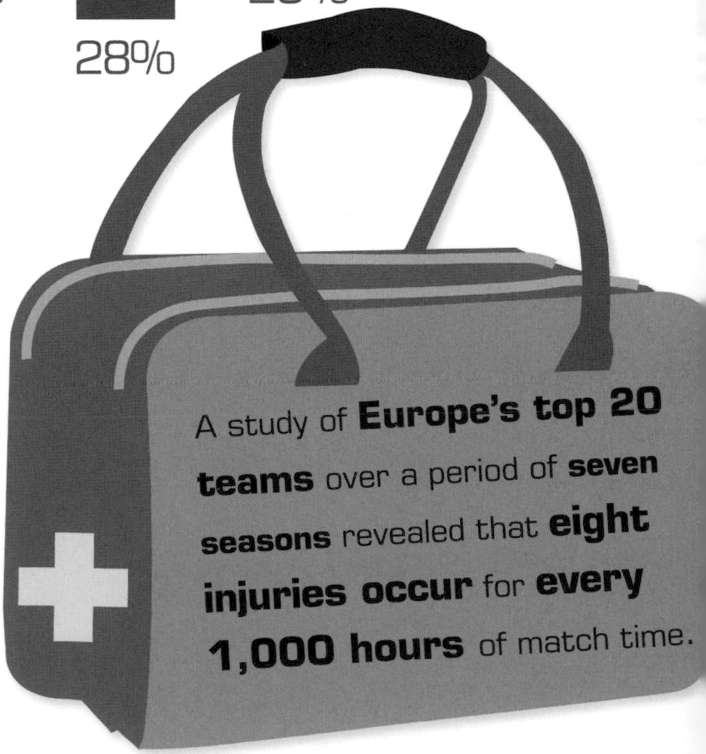

A study of **Europe's top 20 teams** over a period of **seven seasons** revealed that **eight injuries occur** for **every 1,000 hours** of match time.

The **non-European clubs** with the **highest average attendances** are:

Argentina

1

Atlético River Plate
54,000 spectators

India

2

Kerala Blasters
49,111 spectators

India

3

Atlético de Kolkata
45,171 spectators

USA

4

Seattle Founders
43,734 spectators

Mexico

5

Club América
43,583 spectators

The 1950 FIFA World **Cup** match between **Uruguay** and **Brazil** at the **Maracana Stadium** recorded the **highest-ever** attendance:

199,854.

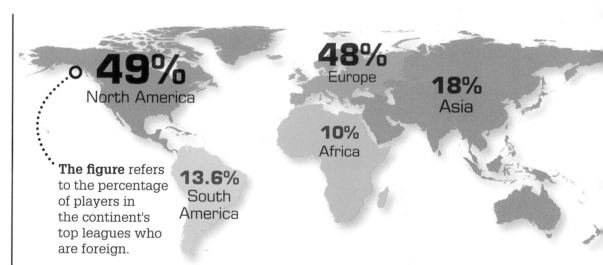

49%
North America

The figure refers to the percentage of players in the continent's top leagues who are foreign.

13.6%
South America

48%
Europe

18%
Asia

10%
Africa

Foreign players in high demand

Almost half of the professional players signed to the top clubs in **North America** and **Europe** are foreign. These clubs are among the richest and attract the world's best players.

Tournaments and trophies

A team's success is measured by the number of tournaments and trophies it has won. At international level, national teams play for the FIFA World Cup every four years. In addition, every continent has its own competition to determine its continental champion at both club and international level.

FIFA World Cup

Played for the first time in 1930, and staged every four years, the FIFA World Cup is the **biggest competition** in football. It decides who becomes the game's **world champion** team.

Diego Maradona confirmed his **status as the world's best player** when he led Argentina to a 3–2 victory over West Germany in the 1986 FIFA World Cup final in the Azteca Stadium, Mexico City.

1970: Brilliant Brazil
Brazil beat Italy 4–1 in the final in Mexico City. This was the first time two former champions had met in the final. It was also the first time a FIFA World Cup tournament was screened in colour.

1982: Inspired Italy
Goals from Paolo Rossi, Marco Tardelli (both above), and Alessandro Altobelli helped Italy to a 3–1 victory over West Germany in a gripping final. Victory saw Italy join Brazil as three-time FIFA World Cup winners.

Only 13 teams contested the first FIFA World Cup in Uruguay in 1930.

COMPETITION FACTS

First played: 1930

Confederation: FIFA

Number of teams: 32

Qualifying to determine the 32-team line-up for the FIFA World Cup usually starts three years before the start of the tournament.

UEFA European Championship

The UEFA European Championship was **first played in 1960** and is staged every four years. It determines the **champion of Europe**.

Despite being called up to play in the tournament as a last-minute replacement, Denmark shocked Germany 2–0 in the 1992 final.

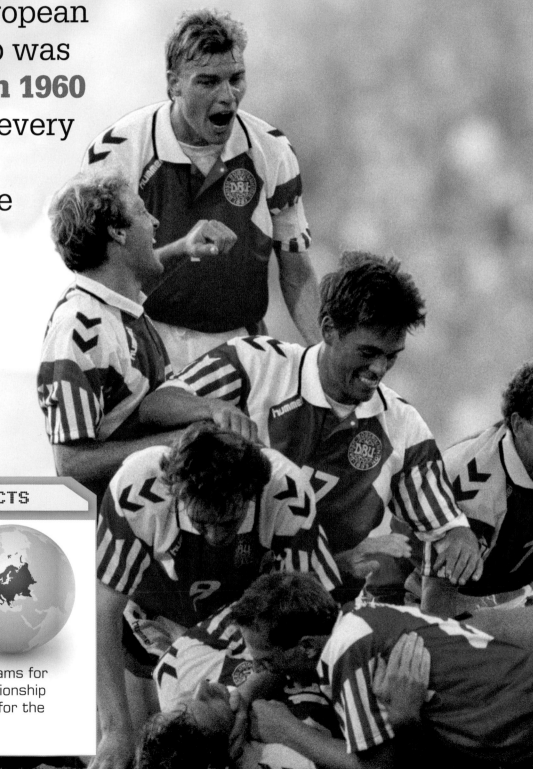

📊 COMPETITION FACTS

First played:
1960

Confederation:
UEFA

Number of teams:
24

The number of qualifying teams for the UEFA European Championship finals was increased to 24 for the first time in 2016.

Spain and **Germany** have both won the tournament on **three** occasions.

TOURNAMENT HIGHLIGHTS

1984: Allez les Bleus
Michel Platini (above) led France to victory on home soil by scoring nine goals in the tournament (a record), including one in France's 2–0 final victory over Spain.

1988: Beautiful orange
Goals from Ruud Gullit and Marco van Basten helped the Netherlands beat the Soviet Union 2–0 in the final. This is the Netherlands' only international tournament victory.

2012: Spanish double
Two goals in each half saw Spain demolish Italy 4–0 in the final to become the first team in the tournament's history to defend their title successfully.

Copa América

The Copa América is the **world's oldest** international football tournament. First staged in 1916 and **held every four years**, it determines the **champion of South America**.

Goalkeeper Claudio Bravo was Chile's hero in the 2016 tournament when he helped his side beat Argentina on penalties. It was the second time Chile had won the tournament.

COMPETITION FACTS

First played:
1916

Confederation:
CONMEBOL

Number of teams:
12

The current format features 12 teams. There is a group stage (three groups of four teams) which is followed by a knockout stage.

TOURNAMENT HIGHLIGHTS

1949: Brazil end 27-year wait
Zizinho (above right) led Brazil as they crushed Paraguay 7—0 in the final. It was Brazil's third Copa América success, but the first time they had won the tournament for 27 years.

1979: Perfect Paraguay
Paraguay beat Chile 3—1 on aggregate in the final (they won 3—0 in the first leg before losing 1—0 in the second) to win the trophy for the second time.

1993: Beyond the boundaries
Argentina beat Mexico 2—1 in the final. This was the first time teams from outside South America (Mexico and the United States) had competed in the tournament.

Brazil and Uruguay have **won** the tournament every time they have been hosts.

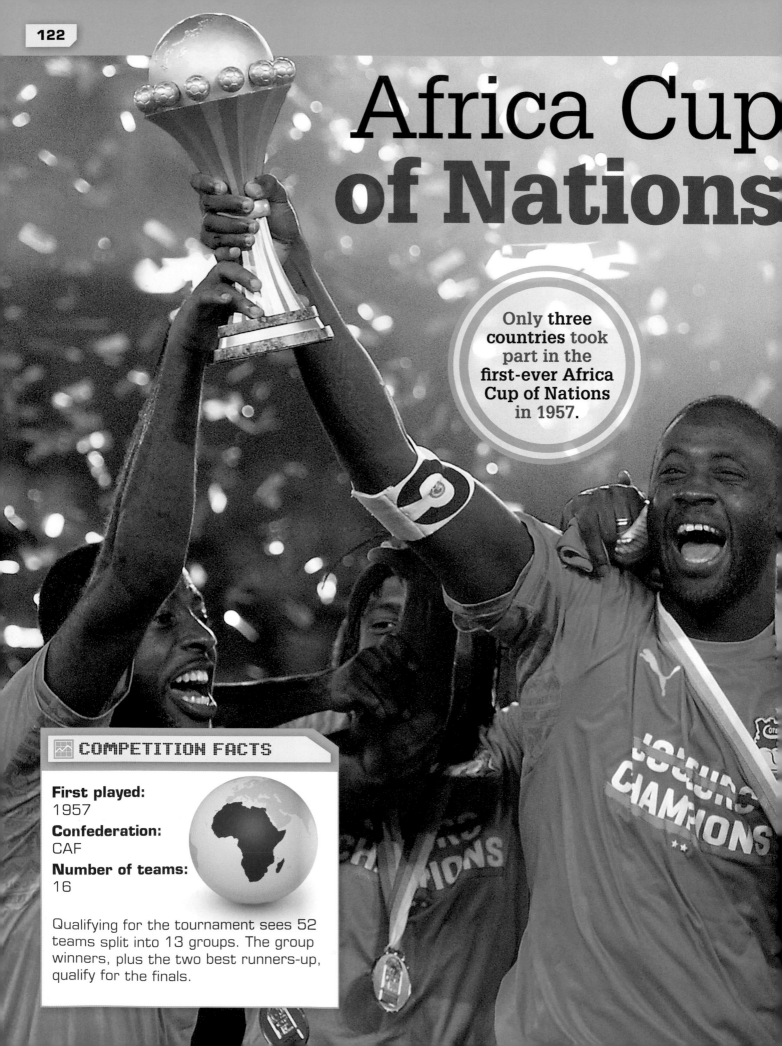

Africa Cup of Nations

Only **three countries** took part in the **first-ever Africa Cup of Nations** in 1957.

📊 COMPETITION FACTS

First played:
1957

Confederation:
CAF

Number of teams:
16

Qualifying for the tournament sees 52 teams split into 13 groups. The group winners, plus the two best runners-up, qualify for the finals.

The **Africa Cup of Nations** is a tournament to decide the **champions of Africa**. It was held for the first time in 1957 and, unlike most other major tournaments, is **staged every two years**.

Having lost the 2006 and 2012 finals on penalties, the Ivory Coast finally ended up on the right side of the penalty shootout lottery when they beat Ghana 9–8 on penalties in the 2015 final.

TOURNAMENT HIGHLIGHTS

1988: Classy Cameroon
Cameroon, led by Roger Milla (above), confirmed their status as Africa's dominant team when they beat Nigeria 1–0 in the final. It was their second title in four years.

1996: Home comforts
Two goals from Mark Williams saw South Africa mark their first appearance in the tournament by beating Tunisia 2–0 in the final in Johannesburg.

2008: Egypt's sensational six
Egypt beat Cameroon 1–0 in the final to win the tournament for the sixth time — a seventh tournament victory followed in 2010.

Hosts Australia, runners-up in 2011, beat South Korea 2–1 after extra-time in the 2015 final in Sydney to win the tournament for the first time.

TOURNAMENT HIGHLIGHTS

1996: Super Saudi
Goalkeeper Mohamed-Al-Deayea (above) helped Saudi Arabia beat the United Arab Emirates 4–2 on penalties in the final, to win the tournament for the third time.

2007: Jakarta joy for Iraq
Iraq put the political turmoil in their own country to one side when they beat Saudi Arabia 1–0 in the final in Jakarta, Indonesia, to win the tournament for the first time.

2011: Fourth title for Japan
A 109th-minute goal from Tadanari Lee saw Japan beat Australia 1–0 in the final in Doha, Qatar, to win the AFC Asian Cup for a record fourth time.

Australia joined the **Asian confederation** in 2007 and **won the tournament in 2015.**

AFC Asia Cup

First contested in 1956, the **AFC Asian Cup** is the **second oldest** continental football championship in the world, after the Copa América. It is **staged every four years.**

📊 COMPETITION FACTS

First played:
1956

Confederation:
AFC

Number of teams:
16

Ten teams from five qualifying groups join the teams that finished first, second, and third in the previous tournament, plus the hosts.

Olympic Games

Men's football was included on the Olympic Games programme for the first time in 1900. Women had to wait until 1996 before they had their own tournament.

COMPETITION FACTS

First played:
1900 (men);
1996 (women)

Number of teams:
16 (men);
12 (women)

The winners of continental age-group tournaments qualify for the men's competition. Women's teams qualify via numerous continental qualifying tournaments.

Football has been played at every summer Olympic Games except 1896 and 1932.

After collecting silver medals in 1984, 1988, and 2012, Brazil finally struck gold at their home Olympic Games in Rio de Janeiro in 2016. They beat Germany 5–4 on penalties in the final.

TOURNAMENT HIGHLIGHTS

1952: Mighty Magyars
Hungary, known as the Mighty Magyars, confirmed their status as the best team in world football when they beat Yugoslavia 2–0 in the final in Helsinki, Finland.

1996: Olympic firsts
The United States won the inaugural women's tournament at the Olympic Games. Nigeria became the first team from Africa to win men's Olympic gold.

2000: Norway strike gold
Norway beat reigning champions the United States 3–2 in the women's Olympic final – the only final in Olympic history to be won by an extra-time golden goal.

FIFA Women's World Cup

The **FIFA Women's World Cup** was held for the **first time in 1991**. A 24-team competition, it is **staged every four years**, and is growing in size, recognition, and status.

The United States beat defending champions Japan 5–2 in the 2015 final, to win the tournament for a record third time.

An unofficial Women's World Cup, won by Denmark, was held in Italy in 1970.

COMPETITION FACTS

First played:
1991

Confederation:
FIFA

Number of teams:
24

Qualifying tournaments are staged in each confederation to determine the 24 teams that qualify for the Women's FIFA World Cup finals.

TOURNAMENT HIGHLIGHTS

1991: First champions
Two goals from Michelle Akers saw the United States beat Norway 2–1 to win the first-ever FIFA Women's World Cup final, staged in Guangzhou, China.

2007: Double gold for Germany
Germany became the first team to defend their world crown as goals from Birgit Prinz and Simone Laudehr helped them to a 2–0 victory over Brazil in the final.

2011: Japan's joy
Japan became the first world champion team from Asia after they beat the United States 3–1 on penalties in the final in Frankfurt, Germany.

TOURNAMENT HIGHLIGHTS

1960: Magnificent Madrid
Alfredo Di Stéfano (three goals) and Ferenc Puskás (two) starred as Real Madrid beat Eintracht Frankfurt 7–3 in the final to record a fifth-successive triumph.

1973: Dutch masters
Ajax beat Juventus 1–0 in the final in Belgrade, Serbia, to become the first team since Real Madrid to win three finals in a row.

1981: Mighty Reds
Liverpool lifted the cup for the third time in five years, beating Real Madrid 1–0 in the final in Paris. Liverpool would triumph again in 1984 and 2005.

A record 360 million viewers tuned in to watch the 2012–13 final on television.

UEFA Champions League

First staged in 1956 and known as the European Cup until 1992, the UEFA Champions League is considered the world's **most important club competition.**

Cristiano Ronaldo (left) celebrates as Real Madrid beat Atlético Madrid 4–1 after extra-time in the 2014 final to claim a record tenth title. This was the first time in the tournament's history that two clubs from the same city contested the final.

COMPETITION FACTS

First played:
1956

Confederation:
UEFA

Number of teams:
78

The top teams from UEFA-qualified countries' domestic leagues qualify for the tournament. The main tournament comprises a 32-team group stage followed by a knockout phase.

Copa Libertadores

Staged for the first time in 1960 and contested annually, the **Copa Libertadores** is a competition to decide the **top club of South America**.

Pelé (right, in white) inspired Brazil's Santos to a second successive title when they beat Argentina's Boca Juniors 5–3 on aggregate in the 1963 final.

COMPETITION FACTS

First played:
1960

Confederation:
CONMEBOL

Number of teams:
38

Teams qualify for the Copa Libertadores by finishing among the top teams in the various domestic competitions held around South America.

Argentine Carlos Bianchi is the only manager to win the trophy four times.

TOURNAMENT HIGHLIGHTS

1996: River Plate at the double
River Plate overturned a 1—0 first-leg deficit to beat Colombia's América 2—1 on aggregate in the final. It was their second title.

2005: Battle of Brazil
São Paulo beat Atlético Paranaense 5—1 on aggregate in the final. This was the first-ever final contested by two teams from Brazil.

2007: Dominant force
Argentina's Boca Juniors reached the final for the fifth time in eight years and beat Brazil's Grêmio 5—0 on aggregate.

Roll of honour

FIFA WORLD CUP

WINNERS

🏆 **1930:** Uruguay

🏆 **1934:** Italy

🏆 **1938:** Italy

🏆 **1950:** Uruguay

🏆 **1954:** West Germany

🏆 **1958:** Brazil

🏆 **1962:** Brazil

🏆 **1966:** England

🏆 **1970:** Brazil

🏆 **1974:** West Germany

🏆 **1978:** Argentina

🏆 **1982:** Italy

🏆 **1986:** Argentina

🏆 **1990:** West Germany

🏆 **1994:** Brazil

🏆 **1998:** France

🏆 **2002:** Brazil

🏆 **2006:** Italy

🏆 **2010:** Spain

🏆 **2014:** Germany

MOST GOALS SCORED IN A MATCH

5 – Oleg Salenko
Russia v Cameroon, **1994**

MOST TOURNAMENT WINS

 Brazil – 5
(1958, 1962, 1970, 1994, 2002)

 Germany – 4
(1954, 1974, 1990, 2014)

 Italy – 4
(1934, 1938, 1982, 2006)

 Uruguay – 2
(1930, 1950)

 Argentina – 2
(1978, 1986)

 England – 1
(1966)

 France – 1
(1998)

 Spain – 1
(2010)

MOST GOALS SCORED IN A **FINAL**

3
Geoff Hurst

England v West Germany, 1966

MOST GOALS IN A TOURNAMENT

⚽ **Just Fontaine – 13**
(France, 1958)

⚽ **Sandor Kocsis – 11**
(Hungary, 1954)

⚽ **Gerd Müller – 10**
(West Germany, 1970)

⚽ **Eusebio – 9**
(Portugal, 1966)

⚽ **Guillermo Stábile – 8**
(Uruguay, 1930)

⚽ **Ronaldo – 8**
(Brazil, 2002)

UEFA EUROPEAN CHAMPIONSHIP

WINNERS

🏆 **1960:** Soviet Union
🏆 **1964:** Spain
🏆 **1968:** Italy
🏆 **1972:** West Germany
🏆 **1976:** Czechoslovakia
🏆 **1980:** West Germany
🏆 **1984:** France
🏆 **1988:** Netherlands
🏆 **1992:** Denmark
🏆 **1996:** Germany
🏆 **2000:** France
🏆 **2004:** Greece
🏆 **2008:** Spain
🏆 **2012:** Spain
🏆 **2016:** Portugal

MOST GOALS
IN A TOURNAMENT

⚽ **Michel Platini – 9** (France, 1984)
⚽ **Antoine Griezmann – 6** (France, 2016)
⚽ **Marco van Basten – 5** (Netherlands, 1988)
⚽ **Alan Shearer – 5** (England, 1996)
⚽ **Patrick Kluivert – 5** (Netherlands, 2000)
⚽ **Savo Milosevic – 5** (Yugoslavia, 2000)
⚽ **Milan Baros – 5** (Czech Republic, 2004)

Fastest **hat-trick**
18
minutes
Michel Platini
(France) scored in the **59th**, **62nd**, and **77th** minutes v Yugoslavia in **1984.**

COPA AMÉRICA

WINNERS

🏆 **1916:** Uruguay
🏆 **1917:** Uruguay
🏆 **1919:** Brazil
🏆 **1920:** Uruguay
🏆 **1921:** Argentina
🏆 **1922:** Brazil
🏆 **1923:** Uruguay
🏆 **1924:** Uruguay
🏆 **1925:** Argentina
🏆 **1926:** Uruguay
🏆 **1927:** Argentina
🏆 **1929:** Argentina
🏆 **1935:** Uruguay
🏆 **1937:** Argentina
🏆 **1939:** Peru
🏆 **1941:** Argentina
🏆 **1942:** Uruguay
🏆 **1945:** Argentina
🏆 **1946:** Argentina
🏆 **1947:** Argentina
🏆 **1949:** Brazil
🏆 **1953:** Paraguay
🏆 **1955:** Argentina
🏆 **1956:** Uruguay
🏆 **1957:** Argentina
🏆 **1959:** Argentina
🏆 **1959:** Uruguay*
🏆 **1963:** Bolivia
🏆 **1967:** Uruguay
🏆 **1975:** Peru
🏆 **1979:** Paraguay
🏆 **1983:** Uruguay
🏆 **1987:** Uruguay
🏆 **1989:** Brazil
🏆 **1991:** Argentina
🏆 **1993:** Argentina
🏆 **1995:** Uruguay
🏆 **1997:** Brazil
🏆 **1999:** Brazil
🏆 **2001:** Colombia
🏆 **2004:** Brazil
🏆 **2007:** Brazil
🏆 **2011:** Uruguay
🏆 **2015:** Chile
🏆 **2016:** Chile

* An extra tournament was held in 1959

MOST WINS
AS A MANAGER
6
Guillermo Stábile
(Argentina)
1941, 1945, 1946, 1947, 1955, 1957

MOST TOURNAMENT
WINS

 **Uruguay** 15
 **Argentina** 14
🇧🇷 **Brazil** 8

AFRICA CUP OF NATIONS

WINNERS

🏆 **1957**: Egypt

🏆 **1959**: Egypt

🏆 **1962**: Ethiopia

🏆 **1963**: Ghana

🏆 **1965**: Ghana

🏆 **1968**: Congo-Kinshasa

🏆 **1970**: Sudan

🏆 **1972**: Congo

🏆 **1974**: Zaire

🏆 **1976**: Morocco

🏆 **1978**: Ghana

🏆 **1980**: Nigeria

🏆 **1982**: Ghana

🏆 **1984**: Cameroon

🏆 **1986**: Egypt

🏆 **1988**: Cameroon

🏆 **1990**: Algeria

🏆 **1992**: Ivory Coast

🏆 **1994**: Nigeria

🏆 **1996**: South Africa

🏆 **1998**: Egypt

🏆 **2000**: Cameroon

🏆 **2002**: Cameroon

🏆 **2004**: Tunisia

🏆 **2006**: Egypt

🏆 **2008**: Egypt

🏆 **2010**: Egypt

🏆 **2012**: Zambia

🏆 **2013**: Nigeria

🏆 **2015**: Ivory Coast

🏆 **2017**: Cameroon

MOST GOALS IN A TOURNAMENT

⚽ **Ndaye Mulamba – 9** (Zaire, 1974)

⚽ **Laurent Pokou – 8** (Ivory Coast, 1970)

⚽ **Hossam Hassan – 7** (Egypt, 1998)

⚽ **Benny McCarthy – 7** (South Africa, 1998)

⚽ **Laurent Pokou – 6** (Ivory Coast, 1968)

⚽ **Hassan El-Shazly – 6** (Egypt, 1963)

AFC ASIA CUP

WINNERS

🏆 **1956**: South Korea

🏆 **1960**: South Korea

🏆 **1964**: Israel

🏆 **1968**: Iran

🏆 **1972**: Iran

🏆 **1976**: Iran

🏆 **1980**: Kuwait

🏆 **1984**: Saudi Arabia

🏆 **1988**: Saudi Arabia

🏆 **1992**: Japan

🏆 **1996**: Saudi Arabia

🏆 **2000**: Japan

🏆 **2004**: Japan

🏆 **2007**: Iraq

🏆 **2011**: Japan

🏆 **2015**: Australia

MOST TOURNAMENT WINS

 Japan 4

 Iran 3

 Saudi Arabia 3

OLYMPIC GAMES

WINNERS

- 1900: Great Britain
- 1904: Canada
- 1908: Great Britain
- 1912: Great Britain
- 1920: Belgium
- 1924: Uruguay
- 1928: Uruguay
- 1932: *No tournament*
- 1936: Italy
- 1948: Sweden
- 1952: Hungary
- 1956: Soviet Union
- 1960: Yugoslavia
- 1964: Hungary
- 1968: Hungary
- 1972: Poland
- 1976: East Germany
- 1980: Czechoslovakia
- 1984: France
- 1988: Soviet Union
- 1992: Spain
- 1996: Nigeria (men); United States (women)
- 2000: Cameroon (men); Norway (women)
- 2004: Argentina (men); United States (women)
- 2008: Argentina (men); United States (women)
- 2012: Mexico (men); United States (women)
- 2016: Brazil (men); Germany (women)

WOMEN: MOST TOURNAMENT WINS

 United States – 4

 Norway – 1

 Germany – 1

WOMEN: MOST GOALS IN A TOURNAMENT

 Christine Sinclair – 6 (Canada, 2012)

Cristiane – 5 (Brazil, 2004 and 2008)

Birgit Prinz – 5 (Germany, 2004)

Melanie Behringer – 5 (Germany, 2016)

MEN: MOST TOURNAMENT WINS

 Great Britain 3

Hungary 3

 Argentina 2

 Soviet Union 2

FIFA WOMEN'S WORLD CUP

WINNERS

- 1991: United States
- 1995: Norway
- 1999: United States
- 2003: Germany
- 2007: Germany
- 2011: Japan
- 2015: United States

MOST GOALS IN A TOURNAMENT

 Michelle Akers – 10 (United States, 1991)

Heidi Mohr – 7 (Germany, 1991)

Sissi – 7 (Brazil, 1999)

Sun Wen – 7 (China, 1999)

Birgit Prinz – 7 (Germany, 2003)

MOST TOURNAMENT WINS

 United States 3

 Germany 2

 Norway 1

 Japan 1

UEFA CHAMPIONS LEAGUE

WINNERS

🏆 **1956**: Real Madrid
🏆 **1957**: Real Madrid
🏆 **1958**: Real Madrid
🏆 **1959**: Real Madrid
🏆 **1960**: Real Madrid
🏆 **1961**: Benfica
🏆 **1962**: Benfica
🏆 **1963**: Milan
🏆 **1964**: Internazionale
🏆 **1965**: Internazionale
🏆 **1966**: Real Madrid
🏆 **1967**: Celtic
🏆 **1968**: Manchester United
🏆 **1969**: Milan
🏆 **1970**: Feyenoord
🏆 **1971**: Ajax
🏆 **1972**: Ajax
🏆 **1973**: Ajax
🏆 **1974**: Bayern Munich
🏆 **1975**: Bayern Munich
🏆 **1976**: Bayern Munich

🏆 **1977**: Liverpool
🏆 **1978**: Liverpool
🏆 **1979**: Nottingham Forest
🏆 **1980**: Nottingham Forest
🏆 **1981**: Liverpool
🏆 **1982**: Aston Villa
🏆 **1983**: Hamburg
🏆 **1984**: Liverpool
🏆 **1985**: Juventus
🏆 **1986**: Steaua Bucharest
🏆 **1987**: Porto
🏆 **1988**: PSV Eindhoven
🏆 **1989**: Milan
🏆 **1990**: Milan
🏆 **1991**: Red Star Belgrade
🏆 **1992**: Barcelona
🏆 **1993**: Marseille
🏆 **1994**: Milan
🏆 **1995**: Ajax
🏆 **1996**: Juventus

🏆 **1997**: Borussia Dortmund
🏆 **1998**: Real Madrid
🏆 **1999**: Manchester United
🏆 **2000**: Real Madrid
🏆 **2001**: Bayern Munich
🏆 **2002**: Real Madrid
🏆 **2003**: Milan
🏆 **2004**: Porto
🏆 **2005**: Liverpool
🏆 **2006**: Barcelona
🏆 **2007**: Milan
🏆 **2008**: Manchester United
🏆 **2009**: Barcelona
🏆 **2010**: Internazionale
🏆 **2011**: Barcelona
🏆 **2012**: Chelsea
🏆 **2013**: Bayern Munich
🏆 **2014**: Real Madrid
🏆 **2015**: Barcelona
🏆 **2016**: Real Madrid

MOST GOALS IN A TOURNAMENT

Cristiano Ronaldo – 17
(Real Madrid, Spain – 2015–16)

Cristiano Ronaldo – 16
(Real Madrid, Spain – 2013–14)

Jose Altafini – 14
(Milan, Italy – 1962–63)

Lionel Messi – 14
(Barcelona, Spain – 2011–12)

Ferenc Puskás – 12
(Real Madrid, Spain – 1959–60)

Gerd Müller – 12
(Bayern Munich, Germany – 1972–73)

Ruud van Nistelrooy – 12
(Manchester United, Netherlands – 2002–03)

Lionel Messi – 12
(Barcelona, Spain – 2010–11)

COPA LIBERTADORES

WINNERS

- 🏆 **1960**: Peñarol
- 🏆 **1961**: Peñarol
- 🏆 **1962**: Santos
- 🏆 **1963**: Santos
- 🏆 **1964**: Independiente
- 🏆 **1965**: Independiente
- 🏆 **1966**: Peñarol
- 🏆 **1967**: Racing
- 🏆 **1968**: Estudiantes
- 🏆 **1969**: Estudiantes
- 🏆 **1970**: Estudiantes
- 🏆 **1971**: Nacional
- 🏆 **1972**: Independiente
- 🏆 **1973**: Independiente
- 🏆 **1974**: Independiente
- 🏆 **1975**: Independiente
- 🏆 **1976**: Cruzeiro
- 🏆 **1977**: Boca Juniors
- 🏆 **1978**: Boca Juniors

- 🏆 **1979**: Olimpia
- 🏆 **1980**: Nacional
- 🏆 **1981**: Flamengo
- 🏆 **1982**: Peñarol
- 🏆 **1983**: Grêmio
- 🏆 **1984**: Independiente
- 🏆 **1985**: Argentinos Juniors
- 🏆 **1986**: River Plate
- 🏆 **1987**: Peñarol
- 🏆 **1988**: Nacional
- 🏆 **1989**: Atlético Nacional
- 🏆 **1990**: Olimpia
- 🏆 **1991**: Colo-Colo
- 🏆 **1992**: São Paulo
- 🏆 **1993**: São Paulo
- 🏆 **1994**: Vélez Sársfield
- 🏆 **1995**: Grêmio
- 🏆 **1996**: River Plate
- 🏆 **1997**: Cruzeiro
- 🏆 **1998**: Vasco da Gama

- 🏆 **1999**: Palmeiras
- 🏆 **2000**: Boca Juniors
- 🏆 **2001**: Boca Juniors
- 🏆 **2002**: Olimpia
- 🏆 **2003**: Boca Juniors
- 🏆 **2004**: Once Caldas
- 🏆 **2005**: São Paulo
- 🏆 **2006**: Internacional
- 🏆 **2007**: Boca Juniors
- 🏆 **2008**: LDU Quito
- 🏆 **2009**: Estudiantes
- 🏆 **2010**: Internacional
- 🏆 **2011**: Santos
- 🏆 **2012**: Corinthians
- 🏆 **2013**: Atlético Mineiro
- 🏆 **2014**: San Lorenzo
- 🏆 **2015**: River Plate
- 🏆 **2016**: Atlético Nacional

MOST GOALS IN A TOURNAMENT

- ⚽ **Daniel Onega – 17**
  (River Plate, Argentina – 1966)
- ⚽ **Luizão – 15**
  (Corinthians, Brazil – 2000)
- ⚽ **Norberto Raffo – 14**
  (Racing, Argentina – 1967)
- ⚽ **Palhinha – 13**
  (Cruzeiro, Brazil – 1976)
- ⚽ **Mário Jardel – 12**
  (Grêmio, Brazil – 1995)

MOST WINS BY COUNTRY:

 24 Argentina

 17 Brazil

 8 Uruguay

 3 Colombia

 3 Paraguay

 1 Chile

 1 Ecuador

MOST TOURNAMENT WINS

Independiente
(Argentina) **– 7**

Boca Juniors
(Argentina) **– 6**

Peñarol
(Uruguay) **– 5**

Estudiantes
(Argentina) **– 4**

GLOSSARY

Here are the meanings of some words relating to football rules, tactics, and equipment.

Added time
The amount of time added at the end of each half to make up for stoppages during the game.

Assist
A pass in a match that directly leads to a goal.

Attacking team
The team that is in possession of the ball.

Away match
A game that is played in the opponent's stadium.

Back four
The four players in front of the goalkeeper who form the defensive line.

Bench
The area next to the pitch in which the team staff and substitutes sit during a match.

Booking
When the referee shows a player a yellow card for a serious offence.

Box-to-box midfielder
A midfielder who plays in both attack and defence, moving from one penalty box to the other.

Byline
The markings along the edge of the pitch between the goalposts and corner flags.

Centre-circle
The circular marking in the middle of the pitch.

Centre-spot
The mark in the middle of the pitch, where the ball is placed during kick-off.

Clean sheet
Describes a result in which a team does not concede a goal in a match.

Clearance
A defensive move in which a player kicks the ball away from goal.

Corner arc
The white arc at each corner of the pitch from which corners are taken.

Cross
A ball kicked from the side of the field, aimed at a teammate in or near the penalty area.

Extra-time
The two additional 15-minute periods played in cup tournaments when the score is still tied after 90 minutes.

Far post
The goalpost furthest from where the ball is in play.

First touch
The first contact a player makes with the ball to control it.

Formation
The arrangement of the different players on a pitch – the formation dictates whether a team plays in an attacking or defensive style.

Goalkick
The method of restarting play when the ball has crossed the goal line when last touched by an attacking player.

Goal line
The line marking between the goal posts; a goal is awarded when the whole ball crosses the goal line.

Handball
An infringement in which a player (other than the goalkeeper) touches the ball with the hand or arm.

Half-time
The 15-minute rest period between the first and second halves.

Hat-trick
Describes the feat of a player who scores three goals in a single match.

Injury time

The time added at the end of each half to make up for time lost to injuries, fouls, substitutions, and other incidents.

Kick-off

The method of starting a match, or restarting play after a goal. Two teammates place the ball on the centre-spot and kick the ball into play.

Man marking

A method of defending set-pieces in which each defender is responsible for watching a specific attacker.

Near post

The goalpost closest to where the ball is in play.

Offside trap

A move in which the back four step forward together in an attempt to put the opposition into an offside position.

Own goal

When a player scores against his own team, usually through an accidental deflection.

Penalty shootout

A method of deciding a winner when scores are still level after extra-time.

Playmaker

A player, typically a midfielder, who controls the team's attacking flow.

Professional foul

A foul deliberately committed to stop the opponent from scoring.

Sending off

A situation in which the referee shows a red card to a player, who must leave the playing field immediately.

Set piece

Refers to the method – either a throw-in, corner, or free kick – used to restart play after an infringement or after the ball has gone out of play.

Substitution

The changing of players during the course of a match. In competitive matches, a team can make up to three substitutions.

Sweeper

An extra defensive player who helps the back four by dealing with any defensive errors.

Technical area

The area outside the touchline from which managers shout instructions to the team during a game.

Throw-in

The method of restarting play when the ball goes over the touchline. It involves throwing the ball back in play while keeping both feet on or outside the touchline.

Touchline

The marking along each side of the pitch that denotes the edge of the playing field.

Wall

The line-up of defenders during a direct free kick, who try to limit the shooting angle of the free-kick taker.

Zonal marking

A defensive system of play in which players are given a specific area to guard.

INDEX

Page numbers in **bold** refer to main entries

ACKNOWLEDGMENTS

Dorling Kindersley would like to thank Carron Brown for the index, Anna Limerick for proofreading, and Nick McCabe for additional advice.

The publisher would like to thank the following for their kind permission to reproduce their photographs:

(Key: a-above; b-below/bottom; c-centre; f-far; l-left; r-right; t-top)

1 Getty Images: Dmytro Aksonov (cb). 2 Dreamstime.com: Tom Wang (tr). Getty Images: Dmytro Aksonov (cr). 3 Alamy Stock Photo: Fredrick Kippe (tc). Getty Images: Dmytro Aksonov (cla); Dmytro Aksonov (bl); Dmytro Aksonov (c); Peter Read Miller / Contributor (tr). 4-5 Dreamstime.com: Tom Wang. 6-7 Dorling Kindersley: Stuart Jackson-Carter | SJC Illustration. 7 123RF.com: Konstantin Kalishko (tl). 8-9 Bridgeman Images: National Football Museum, Manchester, UK. 9 National Football Museum: (tr). 10 123RF.com: alhovik (tr); Richard Thomas (clb). Getty Images: Hulton Archive / Stringer (tl). 10-11 123RF.com: Andrey Kryuchkov (cb). 11 123RF.com: alhovik (clb/ball, crb/ball); Andriy Popov (crb). iStockphoto.com: 4x6 (clb). 12-13 Getty Images: Dmytro Aksonov. 14 Mary Evans Picture Library: Illustrated London News Ltd (tl). 14-15 Rex Shutterstock: Xinhua News Agency. 16 123RF.com: Gordana Damjanovic (clb); yukipon (cb); Christos Georghiou (crb). 18-19 Getty Images: Dmytro Aksonov. 20 Getty Images: Popperfoto (cr). iStockphoto.com: Arkhom1983 (cb). Mary Evans Picture Library: (bc). 20-21 Getty Images: David Price (b). 21 Getty Images: Imagno (ca); Popperfoto (cl, cb, bc). 22-23 KJA-Artists: Jon@KJA-Artists. 23 Pitch Heating Limited: (bc). 24 123RF.com: Olexandr Moroz / alexandrmoroz (cra). SWNS.com Ltd: (bl). 26-27 KJA-Artists: Jon@KJA-artists. 28-29 Nike: (c). 29 iStockphoto.com: richjem (tr). 30-31 KJA-Artists: Jon@KJA-artists. 30 Getty Images: Ian Kington (bc); Visionhaus (cla). 31 Getty Images: Dean Mouhtaropoulos (bc); Jean-Sebastien Evrard / AFP (cr). 32-33 Getty Images: Dmytro Aksonov (background); Matthew Ashton (t). 34-35 123RF.com: Monika Mlynek (Stadium). Fotolia: Fotoedgaras

(Stopwatch). Getty Images: Bernhard Lang. 34 Getty Images: Helios de la Rubia (tl). iStockphoto.com: jamielawton (tc); PeopleImages (tr). 35 Getty Images: Gallo Images - Robbert Koene (tc); Alex Grimm / Bongarts (tr). Rex Shutterstock: Friedmann Vogel (tl). 36 Getty Images: Ben Radford (clb). 38-39 Getty Images: Dmytro Aksonov. 40-41 Rex Shutterstock: Image Source. 41 Rex Shutterstock: Matthew Impey / Wired Photos (crb). 42 Alamy Stock Photo: Reuters (clb). Dreamstime.com: Tungphoto (c). 44-45 Getty Images: Jamie Squire / Staff / Getty Images Sport. 46-47 Getty Images: Dmytro Aksonov / E+. 46 123RF.com: Ogm (bl). 48-49 Photo courtesy GoalControl GmbH. 49 Getty Images: Cameron Spencer / Staff (tr). 50 Catapult: (tl). Dorling Kindersley: Jon@KJA-Artists (tr). 54-55 Getty Images: Dmytro Aksonov. 56-57 Getty Images: Dmytro Aksonov. 57 Getty Images: Dmytro Aksonov (baclground). 58 Getty Images: Dmytro Aksonov (c). 58-59 Getty Images: Dmytro Aksonov. 59 Getty Images: Dani Pozo / Stringer / AFP (bc); Dmytro Aksonov (cr); Dmytro Aksonov (cl). 60 Getty Images: Jean-Yves Ruszniewski / Contributor (clb). 60-61 Getty Images: Dmytro Aksonov. 62-63 Getty Images: Dmytro Aksonov; Dmytro Aksonov (taking the kick). 63 Getty Images: Popperfoto / Contributor (bc). 64-65 Getty Images: Dmytro Aksonov (Background); Dmytro Aksonov (c). 64 Getty Images: Matthias Hangst / Staff (clb). 66-67 Getty Images: Dmytro Aksonov (Background); Dmytro Aksonov (c). 66 Getty Images: Pedro Ugarte / Staff / AFP (cl). 68-69 Getty Images: Dmytro Aksonov (Background); Dmytro Aksonov (b). 72-73 Alamy Stock Photo: Fredrick Kippe. 74-75 Getty Images: Dmytro Aksonov. 74 Getty Images: Drew Hallowell / Stringer (cl). 77 Getty Images: Ullstein Bild / Contributor (tr). 79 Getty Images: STF / Staff / AFP (br). 81 Press Association Images: (tr). 82-83 123RF.com: Monika Mlynek (background). 84 Getty Images: Rolls Press / Popperfoto / Contributor (bc). 84-85 123RF.com: Monika Mlynek. 88-89 123RF.com: Monika Mlynek. 90 Getty Images: Popperfoto / Contributor (tc); Popperfoto / Contributor (cla);

Mondadori Portfolio / Contributor (cra); Popperfoto / Contributor (br). 91 Dorling Kindersley: Adam Brackenbury / Stefan Podhorodecki (r). Getty Images: Matthew Ashton - AMA / Contributor (tl); Jasper Juinen / Staff (ca); Popperfoto / Contributor (clb); VI-Images / Contributor (bl); VI-Images / Contributor (cb). 93 Dreamstime.com: Connie Larsen (br). 94-95 Getty Images: Dmytro Aksonov. 98-99 KJA-Artists: Jon@KJA-Artists. 100-101 Allianz: (ca/all images). 102 Dreamstime.com: Dmitry Rukhlenko (cb). Getty Images: Gary Burchell (crb); Yosuke Tanaka / Aflo (l). 102-103 123RF.com: Andrey Kryuchkov (b). 103 Dreamstime.com: Berean (clb). Getty Images: Creative Crop / Digital Vision (cb); Yosuke Tanaka / Aflo (r). 104-105 Getty Images: Westend61. 104 Rex Shutterstock: Brad Smith / ISI / REX (br). 105 123RF.com: Burak Cakmak (br); Wavebreak Media Ltd (bc). Getty Images: Steve Bardens-FIFA / Contributor / FIFA (tr). Rex Shutterstock: John Dorton / ISI / REX (bl). 106-107 123RF.com: Videodoctor (c). 107 Getty Images: Marcus Brandt / Staff / AFP (br). 108 Getty Images: Stuart MacFarlane / Contributor (clb). 108-109 Dreamstime.com: Libux77 (c). Getty Images: Image Source (b). 110-111 Getty Images: Dmytro Aksonov. 111 Getty Images: Conor Molloy / Contributor (crb). 114-115 Getty Images: Peter Read Miller / Contributor. 116-117 Getty Images: Bob Thomas / Contributor. 116 Getty Images: Popperfoto / Contributor (tl). Rex Shutterstock: Colorsport / REX (cra). 118-119 Getty Images: Shaun Botterill / Staff. 119 Getty Images: Getty Images / Staff (tr); AFP / Stringer (crb); Professional Sport / Contributor (cr). 120-121 Getty Images: Hector Vivas / Stringer. 121 Getty Images: Tim Clary / Staff / AFP (crb); AFP / Getty Images / Staff (cr); Popperfoto / Contributor (tr). 122-123 Getty Images: Liewig Christian / Contributor / Corbis Sport. 123 Getty Images: Gallo Images / Stringer (crb); Mark Thompson / Staff (cr); Bob Thomas / Contributor (tr). 124 Alamy Stock Photo: Reuters (tl). Rex Shutterstock: Jurnasyanto Sukarno / EPA / REX (cl); Stringer / EPA / REX (clb). 124-125 Rex Shutterstock: Paul Miller / Epa /

REX. 126-127 Getty Images: Stuart Franklin - FIFA / Contributor / FIFA 127 Getty Images: Al Bello / Staff (crb); Bob Thomas / Contributor (cr). TopFoto.co.uk: © 2003 Credit:Topham / PA (tr). 128-129 Getty Images: Christopher Morris / Contributor. 129 Getty Images: Tommy Cheng / Staff (tr); Paul Gilham / Staff (cr). Rex Shutterstock: Imago / Back Page Images / REX (crb). 130-131 Getty Images: Matthias Hangst / Staff. 130 Getty Images: VI-Images / Contributor (cl); Rex Shutterstock: Colorsport / REX (clb). TopFoto.co.uk: © PA Photos (tl). 132-133 Getty Images: Popperfoto / Contributor. 133 Getty Images: Vanderlei Almeida / Staff (cr); Jefferson Bernardes / Stringer (br); Sergio Goya / Stringer (tr). 134 135 Dreamstime.com: Donkeyru. 136-187 Dreamstime.com: Donkeyru. 138-139 Dreamstime.com: Donkeyru. 141 iStockphoto.com: Dmytro Aksonov (br)

Cover images: *Front and Back:* **Dreamstime.com:** Agencyby (Trophy icon), Burlesck (Football icon), Kirsty Pargeter (Background) *Front:* 123RF.com: Andres Rodrigu cr, Allan Swart c; **Dreamstime.com** Michaelnivelet c/ (Net), Pixattitude cb; **iStockphoto.com:** Dmytro Aksonov fbr, peepo bl; **Nike:** br; *Back:* **iStockphoto.com:** Dmytro Aksonov r; **KJA-Artists:** Jon@KJA-artists bl; **SWNS.com Ltd:** cla; *Spine:* **iStockphoto.com:** Dmytro Aksonov t

All other images © Dorling Kindersley

For further information see: www.dkimages.com

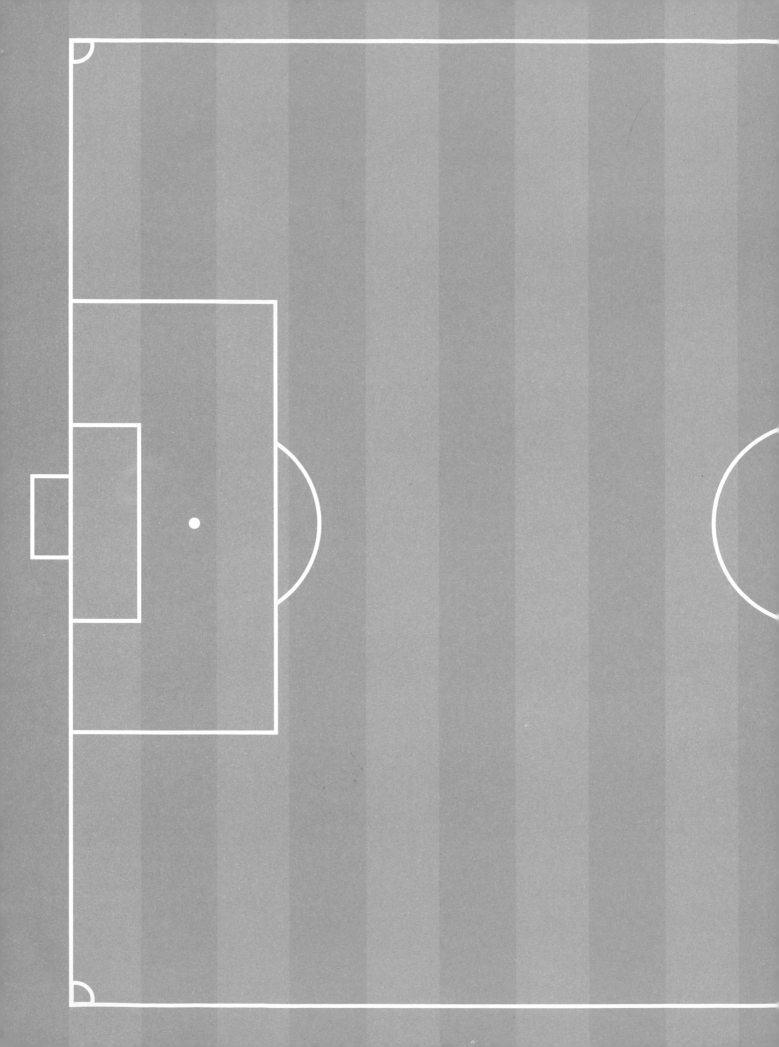